THE CONFIDENT
MOM

OTHER BOOKS BY JOYCE

Battlefield of the Mind*
(over three million copies sold)

God Is Not Mad at You*

Making Good Habits, Breaking
Bad Habits*

Do Yourself a Favor...Forgive*

Power Thoughts*

Living Beyond Your Feelings*

Eat the Cookie...Buy the Shoes*

Never Give Up!

I Dare You

The Penny

The Power of Simple Prayer

The Confident Woman*

Look Great, Feel Great

Approval Addiction*

The Love Revolution*

Any Minute

Start Your New Life Today

21 Ways to Finding Peace and
Happiness

A New Way of Living

Woman to Woman

100 Ways to Simplify Your Life

The Secret to True Happiness

Reduce Me to Love

The Secret Power of Speaking
God's Word

DEVOTIONALS

Love out Loud Devotional

The Confident Woman
Devotional

Hearing from God Each
Morning

New Day, New You Devotional

Battlefield of the Mind
Devotional

Ending Your Day Right*

Starting Your Day Right*

* Also available in Spanish

THE CONFIDENT
MOM

GUIDING YOUR FAMILY WITH GOD'S STRENGTH AND WISDOM

JOYCE MEYER

NEW YORK · BOSTON · NASHVILLE

Unless otherwise noted Scriptures are taken from The Amplified Bible (AMP). The Amplified Bible, Old Testament, copyright © 1965, 1987 by The Zondervan Corporation. The Amplified New Testament, copyright © 1954, 1958, 1987 by The Lockman Foundation. Used by Permission.

Scripture quotations marked (NLT) are taken from the Holy Bible, New Living Translation, Copyright © 1996. Used by permission of Tyndale House Publishers, Inc., Wheaton, Illinois 60189. All rights reserved.

FaithWords
Hachette Book Group
237 Park Avenue
New York, NY 10017

www.faithwords.com

Printed in the United States of America

RRD-C

First Edition: January 2014
10 9 8 7 6 5 4 3 2 1

FaithWords is a division of Hachette Book Group, Inc.
The FaithWords name and logo are trademarks of Hachette Book Group, Inc.

The Hachette Speakers Bureau provides a wide range of authors for speaking events. To find out more, go to www.hachettespeakersbureau.com or call (866) 376-6591.

The publisher is not responsible for websites (or their content) that are not owned by the publisher.

Library of Congress Cataloging-in-Publication Data

Meyer, Joyce, 1943-
   The confident mom : guiding your family with God's strength and wisdom / Joyce Meyer. — First Edition.
      pages cm
   ISBN 978-1-4555-8018-7 (hardcover) — ISBN 978-1-4789-2756-3 (audiobook) — ISBN 978-1-4789-2757-0 (audio download) — ISBN 978-1-4555-8017-0 (ebook) — ISBN 978-1-4555-5324-2 (spanish ebook)   1. Mothers—Religious life.   2. Motherhood—Religious aspects—Christianity.   3. Self-confidence—Religious aspects—Christianity.   I. Title.
   BV4529.18.M485 2014
   248.8'431—dc23
                                                                    2013038682

CONTENTS

CONTENTS

INTRODUCTION

Several years ago, my friend, John Maxwell, was speaking at one of our annual women's conferences, and he opened with a remark that drew a huge response. He said, "Confidence is the uplifting feeling you have before you truly understand the situation."

John was joking, of course, but even so, I think every mother in the crowd could identify with his statement. As moms, we've lived it. Most of us can recall all too well the naïve sense of certainty we first felt at the prospect of motherhood. We can easily remember the idyllic dreams we once had about our soon-to-be-born little bundles of joy.

We also remember when the reality of the situation set in.

Little bundles of joy grew into teething toddlers who cried and threw up on us every time we got dressed up to go out. They threw temper tantrums and tried to drink out of the dog bowl. Soon, instead of feeling sure of ourselves, we started wondering if we really have what it takes to do this right. We started seeing our short-comings, focusing on our failures, and feeling inadequate.

I'm sure you know what I'm talking about. Every mom (no matter how awesomely competent she may appear to be) has lost her confidence at one time or another. But, thank God, there is a way to get your confidence back. It's actually possible for us as mothers, at any stage in our lives, to regain, not the false and fleeting kind of confidence my friend John was talking about, but the real thing: the kind that keeps us looking forward with assurance even when things are going wrong—the kind that keeps us looking up instead of down, in spite of our mistakes. The kind that enables us to laugh at our imperfections and be positive about ourselves and what we *can* do instead of worrying about what we *can't* do.

I'm convinced that right now Christian mothers everywhere are crying out for such confidence. God didn't create us to raise our children under a cloud of insecurity. Insecurity saps our faith. It robs us of our joy. It cheats us out of the boldness we need to really excel at what God has called us to do.

Even professional athletes know this is true. Recently a former basketball great was explaining why some competitors remain average while others excel. He said, "The difference between a good player and a great player is supreme confidence. You cannot lose your confidence!" Although he was talking sports at the time, the same could be said about being a mother—with one important adjustment: The difference between a good mom and a great mom is her supreme confidence *in her supreme God.*

The apostle Paul put it this way: *For we... who worship God in the Spirit, rejoice in Christ Jesus, and have no confidence in the flesh...* (Philippians 3:3 NKJV).

I love that verse, don't you? I like the idea of getting my attention off my own natural flaws and inabilities and putting all my confidence in Jesus! I enjoy my life a lot more when I live that way. I also get greater things accomplished. I've found it's amazing what we can do when we stop struggling to meet life's seemingly impossible demands in our own strength and just lean back on the power and promises of God—because with God, nothing is impossible.

That's why ministry isn't hard for me. It used to be, because I made it hard. I complicated it by pushing myself to be perfect and condemning myself over every mistake. I worried about pleasing other people and wore myself out trying to impress them. But I've come a long way toward giving all that up. These days, I just depend on God and get up every day determined to have a good time in Jesus. As a result, ministering has become easy for me. It's just what I do, and I do it with Jesus helping me all the way.

Though ministry and motherhood are different, they have this in common: They are both divine callings. And when God calls you to do something, He gives you the grace, faith, and anointing (power of the Holy Spirit) to do it. What's more, He sticks with you every step of the way. And helping you get a greater revelation of that reality is what this book is all about.

On the following pages, you won't find a bunch of instructions about how to do everything just right. That's not what I'm here to give you. I'm here to encourage and inspire you with truths from God's Word that will help you be the confident mom you were created to be. By the grace of God, I want to help you shake off the guilt, condemnation, and fear that's holding you back so that you can fully enjoy the unique joys of your calling.

I will warn you in advance, though, the devil will fight you over this revelation. He hates the idea of a confident mom. He's hated it ever since God informed him in the Garden that a woman's seed was going to bruise his head (see Genesis 3:15). That's why he's worked for thousands of years to keep women oppressed. He not only resents what we represent, he understands the powerful influence we mothers have on future generations. He knows there's truth in the old saying, "The hand that rocks the cradle is the hand that rules the world." So he's determined to do everything he can to keep our hands at least a little bit shaky.

But we don't have to let him get away with it. The Word of God proves that—from beginning to end. It gives us one example after another of mothers who trusted God, lived boldly, and overcame the devil's strategies. (We'll talk about some of those moms in this book.) Best of all, God's Word tells the story of the young woman named Mary who gave birth to the Savior. By simple faith in God's promise, she brought forth the Son who dethroned the devil once and for all and provided salvation for all mankind. Christian mothers have been defeating the devil ever since. They've been finding out who they are in Christ, standing in faith on the Word of God, and teaching their children to do the same.

In different aspects of life, mothers are as different as can be. Some are multi-talented homemakers who love to cook, bake, and sew to create beautiful home decor. Others are on-the-go businesswomen who can close a financial deal and help with a science project at the same time. Some have supportive, helpful husbands; others are doing it alone. Some have lots of money to spend on their children; others are barely scraping by.

Today, just as during biblical times, there's no such thing as a stereotypical Christian mom. Victorious, confident mothers come in all varieties and personalities. All it takes is one look at how people who've achieved notable success describe their mothers, and we see how strikingly diverse moms can be:

- Abraham Lincoln said his was as an "angel."
- Andrew Jackson described his as "brave as a lioness."
- Poet Maya Angelou compared hers to "a hurricane in its perfect power."
- Stevie Wonder called his a "sweet flower of love."

Those statements make it clear: You don't have to have a certain kind of personality to be a great mom. You don't have to fit any particular mold to raise kids that wind up literally changing the world. That's good news for all of us because we're each unique. But here's some news that's even better: You don't have to be perfect either. All you have to do is keep growing in your relationship with God and developing supreme confidence in Him.

By His grace, that's something every one of us can do!

CHAPTER 1

Are We Having Fun Yet?

The very idea that the words *Confident Mom* and *Joyce Meyer* could appear together in print anywhere at any time proves two things about God. First: He is, without question, an absolute miracle worker. Second: He has a great sense of humor.

When I first started this journey called motherhood, I didn't have a single shred of confidence. Actually, I was petrified. I felt unprepared, insecure, and inadequate—and I felt that way for good reason!

When I gave birth to my first child, I didn't even know enough to realize what was happening when I went into labor. My husband had left me for another woman early in my pregnancy and, without the money to pay a private physician, I'd been going to a hospital clinic for maternity care. I'd never seen the same doctor twice (actually they were interns) so I'd somehow missed out on the basic information new mothers need.

As a result, for about the first six months after David was born, I was literally afraid of hurting him. It took all the nerve I had just to bathe him. I had no idea how hot his bath water should be, or how hard I could scrub him without hurting him.

If you've heard my story, you already know I had a host of other problems back then too. I was still suffering from the effects of the years of sexual abuse I'd experienced growing up. I was unhappy and totally lacking peace. I felt discouraged and hopeless. Unable to sleep, I'd been taking over-the-counter sleeping pills. Unable to eat, I'd gained only about a half pound the entire time I was pregnant. The strain on my body (coupled with the emotional pressure I was under) left me very sick.

On top of it all, I was broke. I'd held down a job through much of my pregnancy, but when I finally had to quit, I had no way to pay the rent on my small, third-story, garage apartment, which with no air conditioning and no fan was like an oven in the 100-plus degree summer heat. I didn't want to move back in with my parents because of the abusive behavior of my father. So when my hairdresser had compassion on me and offered to let me live with her, I accepted.

Worse yet, when my unfaithful husband showed up at the hospital after the delivery to claim the baby and ask me to take him back, I said yes to that too. Never mind that he was in trouble with the law. Never mind that he had no place to live himself. I agreed anyway to move with him into his sister's house until I could go back to work.

At times it felt like I had nothing going for me, but that wasn't true. I had this one very important thing going for me: At nine years old I had asked Jesus to be my Savior. He came into my heart and—even though I went through times when I felt rejected and abandoned by people—He never left me.

What He's done in my life and in the lives of my children in the many years that have passed since my first terrifying days of motherhood is nothing short of miraculous. Of course, those familiar with my story know that the Lord brought Dave into my life, and he has been a wonderful and loving husband. And today, all four of our children are grown and helping in our ministry in one way or another. They're all talented and amazing. They love the Lord. They're a blessing not only to me but to many others as well. Every one of them is far wiser than I was at their ages. All of them have children of their own now, and they're proving to be great parents.

These days I can truly say I'm thrilled with how my children (and grandchildren!) are turning out. So, by God's grace, I do have a testimony to tell. But even so, it makes me chuckle to think the Lord would lead me to share this book with you. After all, the road to confident motherhood has been a long one for me. I've been anything but a "traditional" mom and I've made plenty of mistakes along the way. So I can tell you with confidence that if God can help me be a good parent, He can do the same for you. I am convinced that He can transform this puzzling, intimidating journey of motherhood into your greatest victory. Better yet, He can teach you to rejoice every step of the way.

Instructions Not Included

Personally, I put a lot of emphasis on rejoicing. I spent so many years being miserable that these days I am determined to enjoy my life. I make no apologies for it either, because I believe it's as important to God as it is to me.

Why else would God include so many verses like these in the Bible?

> ...*I came that they may have and enjoy life, and have it in abundance (to the full, till it overflows).*
>
> John 10:10

> *The kingdom of God is... righteousness and peace and joy in the Holy Spirit.*
>
> Romans 14:17 NKJV

And these things we write to you that your joy may be full.

1 John 1:4 NKJV

Clearly, God wants us as believers to enjoy the life Jesus died to give us. And I believe that He wants every Christian mom to fit the description in Psalm 113:9 of… *a joyful mother of children* (NKJV).

If we're completely honest about it, however, we must admit that many times we don't experience that joy. Although we love our kids and agree in theory that being a mother is one of life's greatest pleasures, the joy of motherhood gets buried under a heavy load of work, worry, and frustration. If someone asks, "Are we having fun yet?" all too often the answer is *no*.

It's not just the day-to-day demands of motherhood that steal our joy (although they can sometimes seem endless and exhausting), but the sense of responsibility we feel for our families. We're aware of how much our children depend on us, and we're often afraid that we're somehow going to fail them—that we don't really know what we're doing. That we don't have what it takes to be everything they need us to be.

As moms, we may not talk about it much but the concerns are there nonetheless. According to one poll taken a few years ago, most parents are their own worst critics.[1] Frequently plagued by feelings of failure:

- They worry that they make too many mistakes.
- They're afraid they won't know how to cope with the problems their kids face.
- They feel like they're not the examples for their children they should be.
- They regret some of the choices they've made as parents and think it's too late to go back and make things right.
- They doubt their ability to relate to their kids and the issues they confront in the world today.

I can sympathize. I've worried about such things myself over the years. Every one of my children is so different from the others and every stage of their development brought such unexpected challenges, I often felt like I'd never figure them out. Oh, how I wished each one had arrived (like household appliances do) with a complete set of operating instructions! God could make things so much easier for all of us moms if He'd just attach to each baby's big toe a booklet that reads: *For*

---

1. Joyce Meyer, "Shaping the Lives of Your Children."

optimum results in infancy, do this... at two years old, do this... during teenage years, do this...

But obviously, He chose not to do it that way—for me, for you, or for anyone else.

Why?

I believe it's because God has a better plan. He wants us to navigate the deep, mysterious, and sometimes stormy waters of motherhood the same way the disciples navigated the tempestuous waters of the Sea of Galilee. (See Mark 4:35-41.) He wants us to stop being afraid and put our faith in Him and His Word, to believe that because we have the God of the universe in our boat, no matter how hard the wind blows or how high the waves rise, we can make it in victory to the other side!

You might say, "But, Joyce, right now I don't feel like I have what it takes to make it through in victory! My toddlers are throwing fits, my older kids are having trouble in school, and my teenagers are rebelling in ways I never expected. By the looks of things, my parenting ship is taking on water and sinking fast."

I understand. I've been there; and I found out there's only one way to stay afloat in those kinds of storms: Take your eyes off your feelings and look to Jesus. Dare to believe that because you're in Him, what Romans 8:37 says is true for you:

Yet amid all these things we are more than conquerors and gain a surpassing victory through Him Who loved us.

What does it mean to be *more than a conqueror*? I believe it means you know in advance you've been divinely equipped to overcome any kind of trouble. It means you can face life with boldness and say, "Nothing in life can defeat me because the Greater One lives in me. He's provided me with everything I need to handle what He has called me to do. I can win every battle because everything I need to overcome them is mine in Christ Jesus. Because I'm in Him, I have what it takes!"

You Have What It Takes

> *It's impossible to enjoy anything when you're afraid of failing at it.*

It's impossible to enjoy anything when you're afraid of failing at it. But once you know with all your heart that you really do have what it takes, being a mom can be a lot more fun. You can do it with joyful confidence and with your own unique style. You can also experience the freedom and joy of helping each of your children be their own unique person.

Picture it for a moment. Think about how fun it would

be to approach every day—not with head drooping and shoulders slumped, focusing on the ways you've fallen short—but letting God be the glory and the lifter of your head (see Psalm 3:3). Imagine having so much confidence in what He's put on the inside of you that when it comes to being a mom, you embrace your role with overwhelming joy and excitement. Well, it all begins when you believe that God has already equipped you with everything you need to be a confident, successful mom.

"I know you're right, Joyce," you might say, "but I don't feel very talented or gifted in my role as a mother. In fact, sometimes I feel like I don't have much to offer at all." If that's you, I want to share some inspiration with you about a mom in the Old Testament who felt a lot like you do—just before she experienced one of the greatest miracles of all time.

The Bible first mentions her in 1 Kings 17:9. There God names her as the person He had chosen to supply food to the prophet Elijah during a drought-induced famine. *Arise, go to Zarephath, which belongs to Sidon,* God told Elijah. *I have commanded a widow there to provide for you.*

From a human perspective, God's plan seemed pretty unreasonable. This widow couldn't even afford to feed her own son—how was she going to feed the prophet? When Elijah shows up at her door, she has nothing and is deeply depressed. So you can imagine how she responded when Elijah asked for some bread.

> *And she said, As the Lord your God lives, I have not a loaf baked but only a handful of meal in the jar and a little oil in the bottle. See, I am gathering two sticks, that I may go in and bake it for me and my son, that we may eat it—and die (v. 12).*

Talk about a mom who felt like she had nothing to offer! This woman tops us all! Yet God saw something in her that she couldn't see in herself. He saw her as a fountain of blessing that, in His hands, would never run dry. Which is why He instructed Elijah to say this to her:

> *Fear not; go and do as you have said. But make me a little cake of [it] first and bring it to me, and afterward prepare some for yourself and your son.*

> *For thus says the Lord, the God of Israel: The jar of meal shall not waste away or the bottle of oil fail until the day that the Lord sends rain on the earth.*

> *She did as Elijah said. And she and he and her household ate for many days.*

The jar of meal was not spent nor did the bottle of oil fail, according to the Word which the Lord spoke through Elijah (vv. 13-16).

Not only is that a wonderful Bible story, it's the story of every Christian mother. All of us realize at one point or another that we don't have enough on our own to meet all our children's needs. In a world filled with danger, we can't guarantee their protection. In a world filled with spiritual darkness, we can't always keep them surrounded with light. In a world filled with questions, we don't have all the answers.

In our own strength, all of us are like the widow in 1 Kings 17—our pantry is pitifully bare.

But even so, we don't have to worry! God has promised to do for us the same thing He did all those years ago in Zarephath. If we'll take a step of faith and give Him what we have, He'll make our lives an ongoing miracle. He'll pour out through us a never-ending supply of His love, His power, and His grace. He'll provide enough, not only for us and our children, but for others too.

So go on and rejoice! Instead of focusing on your own weaknesses and personal shortcomings, celebrate the strength of the One who is in you. Every time the devil threatens to starve your confidence or sink your family's ship, remind him that...

- God Himself has said… *[I will] not in any degree leave you helpless nor forsake nor let [you] down (relax My hold on you)! [Assuredly not!]* (Hebrews 13:5).
- In Christ, God… *always leads us in triumph [as trophies of Christ's victory]* … (2 Corinthians 2:14).
- … *The God and Father of our Lord Jesus Christ… has blessed us in Christ with every spiritual (given by the Holy Spirit) blessing in the heavenly realm!* (Ephesians 1:3).

When you put your faith in God and meditate on verses like those, you'll be able to accept the unique challenges of motherhood with fresh boldness and joy. You'll live like you were born to do this and you're loving every minute of it.

Without hesitation, you'll be able to say, "Oh, yeah, we're definitely having fun now!"

CHAPTER 2

Perfect Women Need Not Apply

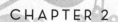

I'd like to be the ideal mother...but I'm too busy raising my kids.

—Unknown

In reality, she doesn't exist. But somewhere in the shadows of most every mother's mind, she is alive, well, and causing major problems.

Her house is always pristine. (No junk drawers for this woman. Everything is organized and stored in attractive, clearly-labeled containers.) Her vegetable garden is an agricultural wonder (organic, of course). She sews like a tailor, does business like a CEO, cooks meals for the poor, and pumps iron daily at the local gym. And she does it all with unfailing patience, sweetness, and smiles.

Some might consider her the Proverbs 31 woman. But the truth is, she's not. The woman in Proverbs 31 has been given to us in Scripture to inspire us. She gives us goals to reach toward by faith and by dependence upon God. But this woman who we strive to be like is a counterfeit designed by our own insecurities that makes us feel inferior and condemned. She's the pie-in-the-sky image of the perfect mom who makes the rest of us feel like failures no matter how hard we try.

She's the reason that in one survey of more than 500 mothers, perfectionism was identified as the number one issue that keeps moms from enjoying the everyday moments of their lives.

And this chapter is all about getting rid of her, because this flawless fictional woman has been undermining moms for far too long. She's caused us too much trouble and cost us too much joy. So there's no question about it: we have to give her the boot and replace her with somebody more scriptural.

The only question is, whom should we choose?

As I've already mentioned, the Proverbs 31 woman is an obvious winner. But there are others in the Bible we might also pick. Women like the ones who appear in the first chapter of the Gospel of Matthew in the passage commonly referred to as *the begats*. (see Matthew 1:1-16 KJV.)

Generally speaking, the begats aren't famous for their inspirational content. But when it comes to providing us with first-rate maternal role models, they're a divinely-inspired gold mine. They reveal exactly what kind of mothers our all-knowing, all-wise God chose to place in Jesus' family tree.

In the begats, we get a picture of the kind of mom through whom God can really work wonders—and it's a picture that doesn't look anywhere close to "ideal."

Take Sarah, for instance. As Abraham's wife, she's mentioned (not by name but by inference) in Matthew 1:2, and she was far from perfect. In fact, she made quite a number of shocking mistakes. If you've read her story, you probably remember some of them.

- She got impatient with God's plan and came up with her own scheme to produce the son He'd promised—she arranged for her husband to have an affair with her maid.
- She got jealous of the maid's son and demanded they both be driven into the wilderness, despite her husband's protests.
- When God showed up again—in Person!—to reconfirm His promise, she literally laughed in disbelief.

Sarah doesn't exactly sound like a candidate for Christian Mother of the Year, does she? Yet God chose her anyway and said, "This is a woman I can work with!" Sure enough, He turned out to be right. Sarah finally believed Him, conceived Isaac, and ended up in the Hebrews 11 *Faith Hall of Fame.*

Then there was Rahab. Mentioned in Matthew 1:5 as another woman in the line of Christ, she first made her appearance in Scripture as a prostitute living in the wicked city of Jericho. Rahab had no Jewish pedigree and no past accomplishments to recommend her. Yet God chose her anyway. "This is a woman I can work with!" He said, and eventually she too found a place in the *Faith Hall of Fame.*

Let's not forget Bathsheba. Bathsheba played a leading role in one of the Bible's greatest scandals. She became King David's wife by way of adultery and got pregnant with an illegitimate child. But instead of rejecting Bathsheba as too flawed to use, God looked at her and said, "This is a woman I can work with!" Bathsheba matured into such a faith-filled, virtuous woman that, according to some scholars, she became the pattern for the woman Solomon wrote about in Proverbs 31.

God Isn't Surprised

I believe moms like Sarah, Rahab, and Bathsheba can be great inspirations. I can identify with the fact that they had flaws and shortcomings. Like everybody else, I've dealt with shortcomings and I've made plenty of mistakes.

Not only was I painfully imperfect in my early years as a mother, when God first called me to start teaching His Word, I was downright embarrassing. I showed up to teach my first Bible studies wearing short-shorts and smoking cigarettes.

I didn't know any better!

But that didn't stop God. He anointed me anyway and those Bible studies succeeded. (Religious minds might have trouble comprehending that, but it's true.) People kept showing up. The numbers kept increasing. God graced me to be a blessing, not because I smoked and dressed inappropriately but because He knew I loved Him and wanted to please Him. He extended great mercy to me because He knew I'd let Him work with me and change me as time went by.

He's still doing the same for me today, and as a mom, you can rest assured He'll do it for you too. He'll anoint you and enable you to be a blessing to your family despite your overflowing junk drawers, gardening failures, and occasional outbursts of impatience. As long as you trust Him to do it, God will help you succeed as a mom and fulfill His plans through you, not because you're perfect, but because He's perfect.

He just asks us to do a few simple things:

1. Receive Jesus Christ as our Lord and Savior.
2. Get to know Him and His Word, and develop a deep, intimate, personal relationship with Him.
3. Lean on Him and trust Him to be our wisdom and strength in every situation we encounter.
4. Follow the leading of the Holy Spirit as He guides us into all truth and continually changes us into the image of Christ.

The good news is that even the things God asks us to do, He also enables us to do by continually offering us His grace. As we lean on Him, we will make progress, but we won't become proud and give ourselves the credit for the success. We will live thankful lives filled with praise for God and His goodness and mercy. Our journey with God is progressive, and fortunately for us, He will be working with us for the rest of our lives.

So we can forget about the pressure of producing a perfect performance. We can get comfortable with making mistakes, admitting them, and moving on. We can know that God always loves us unconditionally and that there is never any condemnation for those who are in Christ (see Romans 8:1). We can live each day in complete confidence and say, "I'm okay and I'm on my way!"

Why do we find it difficult to say things like, "I made a

mistake," or "That's not my strong point," or "I've reached my limit"? Why do we seem perpetually surprised and dismayed over our own natural weaknesses?

God certainly isn't surprised by them.

Just look at what He said in Jeremiah 1:5: *Before I formed you in the womb I knew [and] approved of you [as My chosen instrument], and before you were born I separated and set you apart...* God knew you weren't going to be perfect—only Jesus is perfect—but still He chose you to be His own and called you to do one of the most important jobs on the planet—be a mom. He took your weaknesses into account in advance and made provision for them by sending Jesus to be your merciful and faithful High Priest (see Hebrews 2:17).

For we do not have a High Priest Who is unable to understand and sympathize and have a shared feeling with our weaknesses and infirmities and liability to the assaults of temptation, but One Who has been tempted in every respect as we are, yet without sinning. Let us then fearlessly and confidently and boldly draw near to the throne of grace...that we may receive mercy [for our failures] and find grace to help in good time for every need [appropriate help and well-timed help, coming just when we need it].

Hebrews 4:15-16

Think of it! You actually have a High Priest who understands you. He doesn't require you to be perfect every day in order to have a relationship with Him. And if He doesn't demand perfection from you, you don't have to demand it of yourself either. He does want you to submit the areas of your life to Him that need improvement, but He is there to help you in the process—you don't have to do it all on your own; but you have to cooperate with Him to do the work in your life. You can relax and enjoy your life, knowing that He's pleased with you and He is doing a good work in your life.

Separating Your *Who* from Your *Do*

You might say, "But, Joyce, can I really believe God is pleased with me even though I still mess up and sin sometimes?"

Yes, but to do so, you have to separate your *who* from your *do*. You have to realize that you, as God's child, are a new and wonderful creation. Your spirit has been born again in His image. You have His own nature on the inside of you. When He looks at who you are, He sees the very likeness of Jesus and says of you the same thing He said of Him: *This is My Son, My Beloved, with Whom I am [and have always been] delighted . . .* (Matthew 17:5).

Don't just breeze past this. Let it sink in for a moment:

God is pleased with Jesus and He is just as pleased with you. He's pleased that you love Him and that you want to grow and learn. So dare to believe it. You may even want to stop and say a few times each day, "Even though I'm not perfect, God loves me. He is pleased with me!"

This doesn't mean, however, that God will approve of everything you do. When you do something wrong, He's going to correct you. He'll expect you to repent, accept His forgiveness, and receive from Him the grace you need to change your behavior. But through it all, His love for you and His delight in who you are will remain constant.

As a mother, I understand how that's possible. Not one of my four children do everything the way I'd like them to, but I'm pleased with them nonetheless. I love to spend time with them and talk with them. I love to watch them develop and mature. I'm delighted with who they are. What's more, I won't tolerate anybody coming around telling me what's wrong with them. They're *my* kids and correcting them isn't anyone else's business!

God feels the same way about us. When the devil starts criticizing and heaping condemnation on us, He doesn't want us to put up with it. He wants us to say, "I'm a child of God. I don't have to listen to the accusation of the enemy."

Honestly, we shouldn't even be criticizing ourselves. We can't live with confidence if we're always thinking, *I shouldn't have done that. I shouldn't have said that. I should have prayed more today. I should have spent more time confessing the Word. I shouldn't have been so impatient. I should have given my children more hugs today. I feel so guilty. I'm such a bad parent.*

If those kinds of thoughts are running rampant in your mind, take them captive! (See 2 Corinthians 10:5.) Stop letting the devil criticize every little thing you do and adopt the attitude the apostle Paul had. When people in his day started criticizing him, he said:

> ...It matters very little to me that I should be put on trial by you [on this point], and that you or any other human tribunal should investigate and question and cross-question me. I do not even put myself on trial and judge myself. I am not conscious of anything against myself, and I feel blameless; but I am not vindicated and acquitted before God on that account. It is the Lord [Himself] Who examines and judges me.
>
> 1 Corinthians 4:3-4

Now that's what I call freedom! And it's what God wants for all of us. He wants us to give up the habit of judging and criticizing ourselves. He wants us to say, "I'm determined to do my best each day, but even if I miss it, I'm not going to be filled with worry over it. I'm going to trust God that if I'm doing something that's really displeasing to Him, He'll speak to me and show me how to change it."

God can work with us when we think like that. As long as we love Him, keep walking with Him, and put our faith in His perfection instead of our own, no matter how many mistakes we make or how much we miss it, He'll always get us back on the right path!

Learning How Real People Deal with the Real World

Many times we worry about our mistakes and imperfections because we know our children are watching everything we do. We are extremely aware of the importance of setting a good example for our children to follow. While it is true that you are a role model for your children, you don't have to be perfect to be a good role model.

As a matter of fact, if you willingly acknowledge your mistakes and are quick to repent, if you keep trusting God and refuse to feel condemned, your shortcomings can be a great help to your kids. They can help them learn how real people deal with a real world. They can give your kids the opportunity to see that even though we're all imperfect, we can still receive God's forgiveness and things can work out okay.

That's one of the most valuable lessons children can learn. They need to know that we, as spiritually healthy believers, don't have to hide our faults. We can talk about them openly and share with others what we've learned about how to deal with them. We can be honest about our own humanity and use our mistakes to encourage others and put them at ease.

This isn't just something I preach, it's something I started practicing in my own personal life many years ago. I remember times, for instance, when Dave and I would get into a heated discussion in front of one or all of our children. Children get upset when their parents argue, so there were times when our arguing made them cry. Dave and I were, of course, sorry for our behavior and for upsetting them, but instead of feeling guilty, we used it as an opportunity to teach them a valuable lesson. We told them that people make mistakes and that we were wrong to be angry. We told them about God's forgiveness and our forgiveness toward one another, and then explained to them that in the real world, people sometimes have disagreements and they can work through them and still love one another very much.

Thankfully, Dave and I didn't engage in those kinds of disagreements in front of our children very often. If we had, it could have negatively affected them. They might have started feeling insecure, or even become angry and argumentative themselves.

Children do tend to mirror what they see in their parents, but always remember this: It's what they see *consistently* that really impacts them. So you don't have to worry about every misstep. You don't need to think you're going to mess up your kids every time you make a mistake. Focus on setting a good example for them and I can assure you that they will not be harmed by your occasional mistakes.

Let them see you pray every day. Let them hear you praise God for His faithfulness on a regular basis. Let them watch you stumble, get back up, and go right back to walking in faith and love again. Show your kids by your consistent example how to be confident, not in themselves, but in God.

That's what Kristin Armstrong chose to do.

It wasn't easy for her, though. As she explains in her book *A Work in Progress: An Unfinished Woman's Guide to Grace,* she spent years pushing herself to be perfect... and by all outward appearances she succeeded. She made great grades in school, built a successful career, married an internationally famous athlete, and gave birth to three beautiful kids. She put together a life most women only dream of. But when her marriage eventually failed and ended in divorce, Kristin's seemingly perfect world crumbled.

That's when she realized her former sense of confidence was a sham. "What I'd had was a thin veneer of arrogance over a core of fear," she said. "When my life started to fall apart, I had no coping skills for this lack of perfection. But for me, this time of brokenness became a time of divine liberation. God had been waiting for over 30 years for me to say, 'Hey, can You help me out, here? . . . I can't do this anymore!'"

With that cry, Kristin gave up her drive to be perfect through her own efforts and put God at the helm of her life. She became what she calls "a major renovation project." She took a sledgehammer of God's grace, shattered her self-made shell of superficial perfection, and started following in the footsteps of women of faith like Sarah, Rahab, and Bathsheba.

In other words, she became a woman God could work with. And that's when He really began to transform her life. He opened doors for her to write and share publicly with other mothers what can happen when we stop striving in our own strength to be perfect. "It's not about me anymore or what I can and cannot do," she says. "I don't have to wonder, *Am I good enough?* I know my confidence is in Christ and I am who He created me to be, so whatever I have to offer or say is good enough. It's such a relief and release! And it's the gift I want to give my children."

Amen, Kristin. What better gift could there possibly be?

God will help you succeed as a mom and fulfill His plans through you, not because you're perfect, but because He's perfect.

CHAPTER 3

God Can Handle It

On May 20, 2013, fourth grade teacher Nikki McCurtin gathered a frightened group of students around her and began to read. She doubted they would be able to pay attention. As much as they loved hearing the stories about Aslan, the Lion, from C. S. Lewis's book *The Magician's Nephew* the massive cloud looming on the horizon had the school children on edge.

Most of the students in Nikki's class were already gone. Their parents had picked them up early, anxious to get them home before the storm hit. Only seven of her 27 students were left, their earnest faces upturned toward her as they sat cross-legged on the floor, waiting for her to resume the story. Nikki smiled at them and swallowed hard to clear the emotion from her voice. "Chapter 9," she said.

The Lion was pacing to and fro about that empty land and singing his new song. It was softer and

more lilting than the song by which he had called
up the stars and the sun; a gentle, rippling music.
As he walked and sang the valley grew green with
grass. It spread out from the Lion like a pool...

The students hung on every word. Tuning out the
thunder rumbling outside, they tuned in to the Lion
who sang in the darkness and created life with his voice.
Nikki felt the Holy Spirit hovering in the room. She knew
the children were too young to realize that the Lion in
the story represented God and the empty land the work
of the devil, so she paused and explained how life always
springs out of darkness and, in the end, good always con-
quers evil.

As if on cue, the intercom clicked on. The principal's
voice echoed through the classrooms and the halls. "Take
tornado precautions *now*!"

Within minutes, Nikki, along with the other teachers
in her wing of the school, had shepherded the students
into the bathroom for maximum protection. The lights
flickered overhead. The children Nikki had fallen in love
with this past school year whimpered in terror around
her. Then her cell phone rang. It was her husband, Pres-
ton. He'd been watching the tornado on TV. "It's coming!
It's going to hit you!" he said. Before she could reply the
phone went dead.

The tornado roared in like a freight train. The floor vibrated and the walls shook. The whimpers of the children turned to wails. "God, give me one verse to pray for them!" Nikki screamed.

His answer was instant. Psalm 91:4: *He will cover you with his feathers, and under his wings you will find refuge; his faithfulness will be your shield and rampart* (NIV).

Praying the verse repeatedly at the top of her lungs, Nikki wrapped herself around a little girl like a human shield. She turned her back to the door and braced herself against the fingers of wind that grabbed her, pulling her toward the vortex of the storm. As they threatened to sweep her away, Nikki suddenly felt a stronger Hand pressing against her back with gentle power, holding her in place.

She turned around to see who it was but no one was there. Then she heard God's voice in her heart telling her that she would be okay, that as terrible as the storm might be, He could handle it.

Cinder blocks crumbled and crashed down around her. The roof ripped away overhead and the vacuum created by the twister sucked the air from Nikki's lungs. Gasping for breath she stood up and whirled around to see the tornado right in front of her, a dark swirling monster of dirt and debris.

And then it was gone. Not just the tornado, but everything

else too—*Paradise Towers Elementary School, and mile after mile of Moore, Oklahoma*. Nikki gasped at the devastation and remembered the scenes the Lord had flashed across her mind a couple of days earlier. They'd looked just like this—like a war zone. Nikki had known it was a warning and she and her husband had heeded it and prayed.

Now she knelt among her students, still huddled together amid the rubble. Some were bruised and bleeding but none were critically hurt. Tending to their wounds, she shushed their sobs. "You're alive," she said. "You're alive. It's going to be all right."

Never Alone

As mothers, most of us have never faced what Nikki McCurtin did. We've never had to pray our way through an F5 tornado, and we hopefully will never have to. But I wanted to tell you her story anyway because in some way we can all relate to it.

We all know what it's like to be hit by a storm. To have winds of trouble roar through our lives and rock our world. Sometimes those winds rattle marriages or threaten finances. Other times they bring sickness, disappointment, or emotional pain. But no matter what kind of storms we face, as moms we all want the same thing that Nikki did: To shelter the little ones we love from the turbulence around them and make sure they come through all right.

That isn't easy, even when all we're facing in life is a few scattered showers. But when the really difficult times come, it can seem all but impossible. And this is the simple truth: Difficult times always come. Jesus told us they would. He said in John 16:33 that as long as we live in this world, we will experience trouble, trials, and distresses. And in these days, mothers especially can verify it's true.

According to statistics, many moms in the United States who grew up watching old re-runs of *Leave It to Beaver* and dreaming of a life like June Cleaver's are being blindsided by an entirely different reality. In the past 50 years, divorce rates have doubled. The percentage of families where the woman is the head of the household has risen by a staggering 47 percent. Fewer moms than ever have the option of staying at home with their kids and fewer households earn a comfortable living.

In this day and age, family life is more complicated.

- 61 percent of mothers work outside of the home.
- 86 percent of those mothers say they sometimes or frequently feel stressed.
- 48 percent of all first marriages in America end in divorce.

- 19 million children are being raised by single mothers.
- 51 percent of those children are living below the poverty line.
- 43 percent of marriages are second or third marriages.
- 68 percent of those re-marriages involve children from prior marriages.
- 2,100 new blended families are being formed every day.
- 82 percent of new blended family parents say they don't know where to turn for help for the problems they're facing.[1]

Clearly, times have changed. This isn't June Cleaver's world anymore.

Maybe you already know this from experience. Maybe you've been touched by these statistics in a very personal way and the blissful experience of motherhood you once imagined has taken a less-than-blissful turn. If so, here's a word of encouragement for you: You are not alone.

Not only are there millions of other mothers in the

1. See "Working Mother Statistics," Statistic Brain, http://www .statisticbrain.com/working-mother-statistics/; and "Greg Kaufman, "This Week in Poverty: US Single Mothers—'The Worst Off,'" *The Nation*, December 21, 2012, http://www.thenation.com/blog/ 171886/week-poverty-us-single-mothers-worst.

same boat with you, but as I reminded you in the last chapter, Jesus is in your boat too, and He said:

> ...I will not in any way fail you nor give you up nor leave you without support. [I will] not, [I will] not, [I will] not in any degree leave you helpless nor forsake nor let [you] down (relax My hold on you)! [Assuredly not!].
>
> Hebrews 13:5

You might think, *But I sometimes feel so alone! I pray and ask for God's help, but I don't feel like He's with me—or even in the neighborhood!*

If that's the case, let me encourage you to stop listening to your feelings because they're telling you a lie. Jesus promised to be with you and He is. His very name, Immanuel, means *God with us.*

And some of the last words He said to us before He ascended to heaven were these:

> *His very name,* Immanuel, *means* God with us.

> "...I am with you always, even to the end of the age."
>
> Matthew 28:20 NKJV

That promise that He will be with us "always" means He will be with us as we raise difficult children. He'll be with us if we have to deal with absentee husbands or critical in-laws. He'll be with us as we spend sleepless nights comforting colicky babies or waiting up for wayward teenagers. He'll be with us as we face mountains of laundry, clock in at challenging jobs, and endeavor to bring beauty out of broken situations.

That means you don't have to panic if you're facing some overwhelming storm of trouble. You don't have to wring your hands and say, "I just can't handle this!" Instead you can follow the example of Nikki McCurtin. You can ask God for a Scripture to pray and lean back on Jesus.

He has all power in heaven and earth. He is with you. And He *CAN* handle it!

Finding Help in the Wilderness

Sometimes the trouble that we face is trouble of our own making. It is in these difficult times that we wonder if God will still help us, strengthen us, and be with us. If you are facing such a situation today, I want to encourage you to know God has not given up on you. He is with you and He will give you the strength to overcome any obstacle— even if that obstacle was one of your own making.

If you doubt it, check out the story of the young woman named Hagar in the Old Testament. Hagar was a servant in Abraham's household. She was also the woman who got nominated as "surrogate mom" when Sarah decided Abraham should make a baby by sleeping with someone younger and more fertile than herself.

As a servant, Hagar probably wasn't given much choice in the matter. That's just the way things were done back then. But once she got pregnant with Abraham's child, she did get to choose how she was going to respond to the situation. And she chose poorly. She made an already-bad situation even worse by acting snooty toward Sarah and treating her with contempt.

To put it mildly, Sarah didn't respond well. In fact, she got downright mad. Determined to take Hagar down a few notches, Sarah harassed and humiliated her at every opportunity. So Hagar ran away...to the only place you can run when you live in a tent-city in the Middle East.

The wilderness.

For a young pregnant woman, alone and without provisions, the wilderness is a tough place to live. It's dangerous too. Hagar might well have died out there. But she didn't because God in His great mercy met her there and told her what to do.

Go back to your mistress and [humbly] submit to her control...I will multiply your descendants exceedingly, so that they shall not be numbered for multitude...See now, you are with child and shall bear

*a son, and shall call his name Ishmael [God hears],
because the Lord has heard and paid attention to your
affliction...So she called the name of the Lord Who
spoke to her, You are a God...Who sees me....*

Genesis 16:9-13

The God who sees me. That's a wonderful name for the
Lord! And it was first spoken by a mother caught in a
heart-wrenching situation. A mother who had fallen
prey to bad attitudes and ungodly behavior, just as we all
do from time to time.

Hagar's trouble was partly Abraham and Sarah's fault,
and partly her own. God Himself deserved none of the
blame. But He intervened anyway, poured out His kindness on her, and promised her and her child a fruitful
future.

If God would do that for Hagar in Old Testament
times, can't we as New Testament mothers be even more
certain that God will see and care for us when we find
ourselves in the wilderness? Can't we draw near to Him
with confidence to receive mercy and grace to help in
our time of need, even if our need is a result of our own
bad judgment or behavior?

Yes! Absolutely, we can!

But when we do, we should remember that God won't
always instantly deliver us out of every troublesome situ-

ation. He won't always make our difficulties go *POOF!* and disappear. Just as He sent Hagar back to put up with Sarah for a season, God will often require us to work through our problems over time with His help. And when we tell Him we can't do it, He'll say to us what He said to Paul in 2 Corinthians 12:9: *My grace... is enough for you.*

"Lord, my child's strong-willed personality is too much to handle! It's driving me crazy!"

My grace is enough for you.

"Lord, I know we need the income but I can't stand to work this job another day!"

My grace is enough for you.

"Lord, it's hard being a single parent. I'm too weary to go on!"

My grace is enough for you.

Exactly What Is God's Grace?

Grace is God's power that enables us to do with ease what we could never do on our own. It's His divine favor poured out in our lives supplying us with everything

> *Grace is God's power that enables us to do with ease what we could never do on our own.*

we need. With the help of God's grace, you and I can accomplish things that would have been impossible for us to do on our own, no matter how hard we struggled and tried.

And because God dispenses grace to us in abundance according to our need, grace is the great equalizer! The more problems and weaknesses you have, the more grace you get!

"But you don't know my situation," you might say. "You've never had to deal with the kinds of things I do."

I'm sure that's true. We all have our own race to run and our own storms to conquer. When God called me into ministry, I had three teenagers at home and a baby that I often carried on my hip while trying to do God's will. I had to deal with a father who'd sexually abused me for years as a child and still refused to acknowledge he was wrong, and a mother who was in complete denial. I was dealing with friends and family who had completely rejected me because I was teaching God's Word and in their opinion, "Women can't do that!" I also had a variety of minor health issues due to the stress I had been under for a long period of time.

What's more, while I was traveling and teaching the Word and trying to be a good mother, wife, and homemaker all at the same time, my husband wasn't acting the way I thought he should. He insisted on using his free time to play golf or watch football on television instead of catering to me. I tried everything I knew to change him. I pouted. I argued. I manipulated. I even begged God to convict him! But God didn't do it my way. Apparently He wanted me to focus on my own walk with Him and not Dave's. So instead of making Dave do what I wanted him to do, God gave me extra grace to let Him change me and to trust Him with everything and everyone else. I would love to say that it happened dramatically and quickly, but honestly, it took a lot longer than I wanted it to; however, God ultimately used the things that were difficult for me to handle so He could change me and bring me into a deeper and more intimate relationship with Him.

That's my story. Yours may be very different. The challenges we face are all unique and very different. But even so, you can count on this: God will give you more than enough grace to handle them. If you're a single mom, raising several children on your own and working full-time to pay the bills, God will fill you to the brim with grace enough to do it all with joy and peace. If you're a stay-at-home mom and you're feeling cut off from the world and unfruitful in God's kingdom, He'll do the same, supplying you with His grace in your time of need. God promises to give each of us . . .

- More and more grace (see James 4:6).
- *...One grace after another and spiritual blessing upon spiritual blessing and even favor upon favor and gift [heaped] upon gift* (John 1:16).
- A surpassing measure of God's grace (see 2 Corinthians 9:14).

I saw an example of this in the life of my daughter, Sandra. After her twins were born, the Lord led her to give up working in our ministry and stay home full-time. She knew it was the right decision at the time and, like all moms with young toddlers, she stayed very busy. But even so, she still yearned to reach out to others with the Word of God. So she asked God for extra grace. She prayed each day with her two-year-old daughters that He would make them a light everywhere they went.

Sure enough, He did it! God gave Sandra inspired ideas and the boldness to act on them. One time, for instance, she decided to encourage and appreciate the garbage man. She wrote him a thank-you note and enclosed $50. She told him to treat himself to a nice lunch and gave him one of my books. Another time, she was driving down the street and noticed some bikers gathered in a parking lot. At the prompting of the Lord, she pulled over, talked to them, and gave them a set of my teaching CDs.

Open a Can of Miracles

Some of you may know more about God's grace than I did as a young mom. The first few years I tried to live for God, I didn't have a clue about it. I knew I'd been saved by grace through faith, but I thought that once I was born again, I had to do everything in my own strength. I felt like God threw me the football and expected me to make the touchdown. Oh, what agony that was!

The more I studied the Word, the more I saw all the things that were wrong with me, but I couldn't seem to find the power to change them. I'd hear a good sermon about how I should live and what I needed to do. I'd agree with it, try to act on it, and fall flat on my face. I'd read a good Christian book, see where I was falling short, and then go right out and fall short again. All this trying and failing only made me more frustrated than I already was, and it often caused me to be grouchy with my children.

But, thankfully, with the help of the Lord, I finally began to learn how to receive God's grace. I stopped struggling in the flesh, started acknowledging my utter dependence on God, and trusted Him to do through me the things I cannot do on my own.

Somebody once said, "Miracles come in cans," and I agree. Miracles started happening to me when I stopped saying things like, "I *can't* take this anymore!" and started confessing by faith, "I *can* do all things through Christ who strengthens me. Without Him I am nothing, but with Him I *can* do whatever He calls me to do. Nothing is impossible for Him. He *can* do anything and His power is in me!"

I still say those things—several times a day—most every day. It helps me worship God and activate the overcoming power of His grace in my life. It will do the same for you. So if you aren't already doing it, get started. Get into the habit of trusting God and singing His praises all the time. Start saying, "I can do whatever I need to do in life through Christ who is my Strength."

Practice believing His Word and depending on His power even during the sunny days of life. If you'll learn to do this, you'll be ready when the winds of trouble blow and you won't have to panic. You'll know that because of the grace of God, light always overcomes darkness, and good always overcomes evil in the lives of those who trust the Lord. You'll be able to shelter your little ones with your shield of faith and say, "Everything is going to be okay. You don't have to worry about the storm. The Lion of Judah is right here with us…and He can handle it."

CHAPTER 4

Fill 'er Up!

A group of elementary school children were once asked this question: "What did God use to make mothers?" Their collective answer was classic.

"Clouds, angel hair, and everything nice in the world...with a little dab of mean."

Back when my kids were little, they might not have gone along with the clouds and angel hair part of that answer. I do suspect, though, that they would have agreed with the *little dab of mean*. They definitely had reason to. During my first decade or so as a mom (maybe even a little longer than that), I had a tendency to be what you might call "grouchy."

I didn't mean to be that way, of course. I love my kids just like all mothers do. So I always wanted to be patient and kind with them. Sometimes I was. But other times, I was just the opposite. Kind of like a maternal version of Dr. Jekyll and Mr. Hyde.

I tried to change myself; I really, really tried. And if the poets are to be believed, I should have been able to do it. On Hallmark cards and such they often claim the love of a mother is the greatest, most unconditional, infinite love that exists. But as nice as that sounds, I can testify from personal experience, it's not true. Human love, even when it's coming from a mother, has its limits.

And I hit those limits a lot.

I probably hit them a little more often than other moms might because my emotional life was such a mess. Due to the years of abuse I experienced growing up, I was easily angered, and I felt frustrated much of the time. My mood could swing erratically from good to bad.

I knew there was a better way to live because I'd heard plenty of sermons about love in church. I'd also seen in the Bible how real love, the God-kind-of-love (which is far superior to natural mom-kind-of-love) behaves. As 1 Corinthians 13: 4-5, 7-8 says:

> *Love endures long and is patient and kind … it is not*
> *rude (unmannerly) and does not act unbecomingly.*
> *Love (God's love in us) does not insist on its own rights*
> *or its own way, for it is not self-seeking; it is not touchy*
> *or fretful or resentful; it takes no account of the evil*
> *done to it [it pays no attention to a suffered wrong].*

Love bears up under anything and everything that comes, is ever ready to believe the best of every person, its hopes are fadeless under all circumstances, and it endures everything [without weakening]. Love never fails....

Although I was still new in the things of God when I first read those verses, I wanted with all my heart to live them. I expected to do it too. After all, as a Christian I'm one of those people Romans 5:5 is talking about when it says *God's love has been poured out in our hearts through the Holy Spirit Who has been given to us.*

But things didn't go as I expected.

While the kids were in school, I'd spend time listening to teaching tapes, praising the Lord, and getting very spiritual. And as long as I was alone in the house, I was as loving as can be. (Have you ever noticed how much easier it is to love others when you're by yourself?) When the kids got home I'd be singing praise songs at the kitchen sink. But then they'd start slamming doors and dropping books and the praise songs would stop. Suddenly I'd explode in irritation. "What's wrong with you kids?! Why can't you be more careful? Blah...Blah...Blah!"

I felt awful about it, but it kept happening again and again. I couldn't figure out what the problem was. Then one day the Lord explained it to me. "Joyce," He said, "you walk around all day feeling bad about yourself and the pressure of it builds up so much steam inside you that the least little thing can set you off!"

I knew exactly what He meant. My mother had a pressure cooker when I was a little girl. It had a little metal disk on the top that would start jiggling and sizzling when it got hot. If I got close to it, my mother would say, "Don't touch it! It might blow up!"

That's the way I was with my children back then. It's like I was walking around with one of those little metal things on top of my head, jiggling and sizzling. All the kids had to do was annoy me in some small way and I'd blow up, because deep down, I felt so bad about myself.

And why did I feel bad about myself?

One simple reason: I didn't yet have a complete and personal revelation of how much God loves me.

You Can't Give Away What You Don't Have

Even though I was listening to teachings and reading about love in the Bible, I was still struggling with my understanding of God's love. You see, I was mostly focused on what the Bible says about how we should love others. I concentrated on what it teaches us about giving love away. What I didn't realize was this:

It's impossible to give away something you don't have. So to give God's love to others, I needed to receive it myself first. That was something I hadn't done. Even though I was saved and I'd

It's impossible to give away something you don't have. So to give God's love to others, I needed to receive it myself first.

attempted to have a relationship with God, my fellowship with Him had been dysfunctional. I hadn't known how to receive His love, or anyone else's for that matter. That's why—as much as I yearned to walk consistently in the God-kind-of-love, not only toward my children but also toward my husband, my relatives, my neighbors, and even my enemies—I couldn't put together a thimbleful of a decent love walk.

When God showed me what the problem was, I decided to do something about it. I spent an entire year studying and confessing what the Bible says about how much God loves me. During that year, I made it my primary goal to get firmly grounded on the foundation of His love. I spent time with the Lord purposely accepting His love by faith, and throughout the day I affirmed it over and over. I probably said 100 times a day, "God loves me!" I didn't necessarily feel any different at first. But over time God's love became a reality to me.

Maybe I was an especially difficult case. Because of everything I've been through, maybe I had to work harder at receiving God's love than other Christian moms do. But even so, the basic principle I discovered is true for all mothers: If we want to pour out God's love into the lives of our children, we must first receive it for ourselves.

In other words, if we don't want to run out of gas when the road gets steep as the journey of motherhood seems long, we'd better pull into God's love station every day and say, "Here I am, Lord. Fill 'er up!"

The Best Thing You Can Do for Your Family

I know what you're probably thinking. You're trying to figure out how you're supposed to do this. As a mom, your schedule is already packed solid. How are you going to find the time to go to God and get filled up? You're like the woman in the cartoon who's consulting a psychologist for help. "Let's see," he says to her. "You spend 50 percent of your energy on your husband, 50 percent on your children, and 50 percent on your job. I think I see your problem."

That cartoon is not only good for a chuckle, it makes a great point. When moms spend all of their time—and more—on everybody else and take no time for themselves, they start having problems. I see it happen all the time, not just with mothers but with ministers too. They're so dedicated to meeting the needs of other people that they ignore their own needs. After a while, they begin to break down.

Sometimes they push themselves too much physically. They feel like they have so much to do they don't take time to exercise and rest their bodies properly. Eventually, they get sidelined by fatigue, weakness, or sickness. Then everybody who depends on them suffers.

In my ministry, I've invested a lot of time encouraging believers to take care of their bodies. "It's the house you live in." I tell them. "If you destroy it, you have to leave!" Yet as important as physical health is, spiritual well-being is even more vital. You cannot do what God has called you to do without taking daily time to tend to it. That's why as a mom the best thing you can do for your family is take time each day to fellowship with God. (We'll talk about this more in the following chapters.)

> *That's why as a mom the best thing you can do for your family is take time each day to fellowship with God.*

I know it's not easy. I know your children may want all of your attention all the time. But you can only give them the kind of attention they really need if you put your relationship with the Lord first.

One mom from Texas who recently shared her story would add a hearty amen to this. She decided 30 years ago that her children would be far better off if she dedicated the first hour of her day every day to God. At the time, her schedule was already hectic. She had a child in kindergarten, one in elementary school, and a stepchild in middle school. She also worked full-time and taught Sunday School. On top of all that, her husband traveled a lot and most of the household chores fell to her.

The only place she could find in her house to get alone with God was her bedroom closet. So that's where she went early each morning, with Bible in hand, to pray. Because the devil fights us harder over our personal time with God than anything else, what happened next is no surprise. A pipe beneath the closet sprung a slow leak and perpetually soaked the carpeted floor. Although her landlord waited weeks to fix the leak, this mom refused to be stopped. She simply spread a big plastic garbage bag over the soggy carpet and continued to pray.

When she first started those prayer times, the family was a mess. Financial tensions and the stress of a blended family had left her harried and short-tempered. None of the children were interested at all in God and the older ones were beginning to have serious problems.

But little by little, things began to change. As this mom spent time receiving God's love for herself, the atmosphere in her home warmed and softened. Her patience and joy increased. Although she was still far from perfect, the new kind of love her children saw in her profoundly affected them. Soon they were all saved and in love with the Lord.

Today they still are. They're following her example and raising her grandchildren in the ways of the Lord. When she goes to church on Sunday and looks up at the pastor standing behind the pulpit, she's especially glad she spent all those hours fellowshipping with God receiving His love...because now her pastor is her son.

Countless mothers across this nation and around the world have similar stories to share. Each one of them would undoubtedly assure you that you shouldn't feel guilty about taking time from your busy schedule to get alone with the Lord and receive His love. It's the most valuable investment in your family you could ever make.

A Supernatural Cycle

I like the term *investment* because it represents a cycle of input, return, and continual increase. That's what the cycle of God's love is like: He invested His love in you by sending Jesus. When we invest the time to receive that love and love Him in return, the love inside you increases. You start seeing *you* differently and you're more able to love yourself. (That's a good thing! Jesus told you to love your neighbor as you love yourself, right?) You also have more love to give to others. Because God's love is abounding within you, you can love everybody around you like Jesus does.

First John 4:10, 16-17 puts it this way:

> *In this is love: not that we loved God, but that He loved us and sent His Son to be the propitiation (the atoning sacrifice) for our sins. And we know (understand, recognize, are conscious of, by observation and by experience) and believe (adhere to and put faith in and rely on) the love God cherishes for us. God is love, and he who dwells and continues in love dwells and continues in God, and God dwells and continues in him. In this [union and communion with Him] love is brought to completion and attains perfection with us…because as He is, so are we in this world.*

When you're living in this cycle of love and your son breaks a window playing baseball or your daughter spills fingernail polish on the carpet, you don't have to blow your stack like a pressure cooker. You can do something very different. You can let the love of God that's in you flow like a river and bring peace to the situation. You can bring the correction you need to bring without over-correcting in anger. You can be so supernaturally patient and kind that your kids will think, *Wow, Mom … What happened to you?*

So give yourself permission to be like the disciple John. He made such a habit of getting close to Jesus that he actually called himself "the disciple whom Jesus loved" (John 13:23 NIV). At the Last Supper, he was the one leaning against Jesus' chest.

Every mother needs time to herself to lean on Jesus. We all need to refill our hearts continually with the revelation that we are deeply, dearly, loved by God. And, as busy as you are, you're no exception. You need to be reminded daily that…

- God so greatly loved and dearly prized you that He gave up His only begotten Son, so that you could believe in Him and not perish but have eternal life (John 3:16).
- Jesus loves you just like the Father loves Him (John 15:9).
- No one has greater love or stronger affection than to lay down his own life for his friends—and that's what Jesus has done for you! (John 15:13).
- Your heavenly Father Himself tenderly loves you, not because you do everything perfectly but simply

because you have loved Jesus and have believed
that He came from the Father (John 16:27).

- The Father loves you just as much as He loves Jesus
  (John 17:23).
- God proved His love for you by the fact that while
  you were still a sinner, Christ died for you (Romans
  5:8).
- Nothing can ever separate you from the love of
  God, which is in Christ Jesus our Lord (Romans
  8:38-39).
- The Father has such an incredible quality of love
  for you that He chose you to be His very own child
  (1 John 3:1).

These are just a few of the Scriptures that talk about
how much God loves you. I encourage you to use them
to launch into your own study about His love. Take some
time to get in the Word and get close to Jesus. Lean back
on Him and say, "Here I am, Lord. Fill 'er up!"

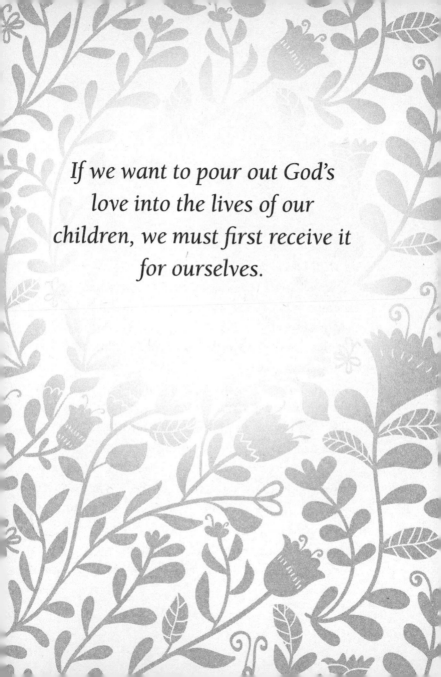

If we want to pour out God's love into the lives of our children, we must first receive it for ourselves.

CHAPTER 5

Keep Your Eye on the Mirror

What would Jesus do?

A few years ago, that was a popular question. It seemed like people everywhere were asking it, and many people even wore bracelets with WWJD on them, or had bumper stickers with those initials representing the question, "What would Jesus do?" You don't hear it as much these days, but while working on this book, I realized it's a great question for Christian moms. It really sums up most everything we need to know.

When our kids are misbehaving and none of our disciplinary tactics have worked, we need to know what Jesus would do to straighten things out. When we only have one nerve left and one of our children is stomping on it, we need to know what Jesus would do to stay sane. When we look at the dangers around us and worry that God won't protect our little ones, or we wonder how to set a good example for our kids to follow, we need to know what Jesus would do in our place.

Just imagine for a moment what a great parent Jesus would be!

- He would be confident in His ability to discipline properly because He has the wisdom of God.
- He'd always be patient because He's full of the fruit of the Spirit.
- He'd always trust God for protection because He lives by faith.
- He'd be a good example 24/7 because He's the perfect imprint and very image of God.

"That's true," you might say, "and it's all well and good for Jesus. But I don't see how that helps me. I don't have all the wonderful qualities He has. *I'm not like Him!*"

Yes.

You.

Are.

If you've received Jesus as your Savior, you have within you everything He is and everything He has. Through the miracle of the new birth, He has been reproduced on the inside of you. That's not just my opinion. It's what the New Testament says. In verse after verse it declares:

You've been recreated in Jesus' image, *regenerated (born again), not from a mortal origin (seed, sperm), but from one that is immortal by the ever living and lasting Word of God.*

1 Peter 1:23

You are *united to the Lord* and you *are one spirit with Him.*

1 Corinthians 6:17

You've *become sharers (partakers) of the divine nature.*

2 Peter 1:4

You are *born of the Spirit,* and *the fruit of the [Holy] Spirit [the work which His presence within accomplishes] is love, joy (gladness), peace, patience (an even temper, forbearance), kindness, goodness (benevolence), faithfulness, gentleness (meekness, humility), self-control (self-restraint, continence).*

John 3:8, Galatians 5:22-23

You *have the mind of Christ (the Messiah) and do hold the thoughts (feelings and purposes) of His heart.*

1 Corinthians 2:16

*For in Him the whole fullness of Deity (the Godhead)
continues to dwell in bodily form [giving complete
expression of the divine nature]. And you are in Him,
made full and having come to fullness of life [in Christ
you too are filled with the Godhead—Father, Son and
Holy Spirit—and reach full spiritual stature].*

Colossians 2:9-10

I know what you're probably thinking: *If all those things
are true about me, then why do I have so many struggles?
Why do I so often end up doing what Jesus* **wouldn't** *do?*

Because the part of you that's like Him—your spirit—
is hidden on the inside of you. It's wrapped up, so to
speak, inside your soul and your body. (This is important to remember: You *are* a spirit; you *have* a soul; and
you *live in* a body.) Your soul and body haven't been recreated like your spirit was when you were born again.
They haven't yet been changed into the image of Jesus.
They have to be transformed (completely changed) over
time until they conform to and reflect the real inner you.

This transformation can be a challenging process. The
first important thing to do is believe that you have God's
nature abiding in you. What you believe determines how
you live, so what you believe is extremely important.
Secondly, remember that transformation is a process.

Celebrate your victories even if they are small—look at how far you have come in your growth in God and don't stress-out over how far you think you still have to go. We'll be working with the Holy Spirit for the rest of our lives, learning how to surrender to His will instead of going our own emotional and stubborn way. We can, however, speed it along by doing something that we as women tend to be quite good at: Looking in the mirror—*a lot*!

Two Life-Changing Revelations

Before you get too excited, let me clarify. I'm not talking about looking in the kind of mirror that hangs over your bathroom sink. That won't do much to make you more like Jesus. If it did, most of us would be super saints already because we've spent countless hours looking into those kinds of mirrors. I know I certainly have. I don't just roll out of bed looking the way you see me when I'm on television or teaching at conferences.

I spend time every morning digging through bags full of makeup, dabbing creams on my face, and squirting my hair with all different kinds of sprays. I like to look my best when I go out, so I consider my natural mirror to be a very important daily tool in my life.

I have another mirror, however, that's far more important to me. It's a spiritual mirror that has changed not just the way I look, but the way I live. It's a mirror that has transformed me from the inside out and given me a whole new life.

In case you haven't figured it out already, I'm talking about the mirror of God's Word.

Although it's sad to say, I lived for years as a mother and as a Christian without ever discovering that mirror. Oh, I read the Bible sometimes. There were even seasons when I would read a chapter every day. But I did it out of a sense of religious obligation. I thought I was doing it for God and He was going to give me brownie points for it. Finally, though, the Lord straightened out my perspective. He said, "Joyce, it doesn't help *Me* when you read the Bible. It helps *you*!"

Exactly how does the Word help us?

It works in many different ways, but when we approach the Word of God like a mirror, it changes us by revealing two things: First, it shows us who we are in Christ. It opens our eyes to our true spiritual identity. Second, it shows us what changes we need to make by God's grace in our attitudes and actions so that our outside can more closely match our inside. In other words, it reveals to us how to live like who we've been created to be.

If you've ever watched the animated Disney movie *Tarzan* with your kids, you've seen a good illustration of what this kind of revelation can do. (Yes, I know Tarzan wasn't a Christian, but humor me here.) Think about what happened in that movie. In the beginning, Tarzan's parents died and he lost touch with his identity. The gorillas in the jungle took him in and raised him as one of their own. As a result, he identified with them and acted like them.

Then he encountered human beings and his life started to change. The more he saw how humans lived and behaved, the more he saw himself in them. It dawned on him that he wasn't a gorilla at all! He was a whole different species of being with the capacity to live an entirely different kind of life. As a result, he began to act differently. He began to live out his true identity. Instead of acting like a gorilla, he began to act like a man!

In a sense, that's what happens as Christians look into the Word of God. Because Jesus is the Word made flesh, we see Him on every page of the Bible. (See John 1:14.) We see who He is, how He thinks, and how He acts. We see in Him who we've been born again to be. In the process, it dawns on us more and more that what the Bible says about us is actually, literally true!

If any person is [ingrafted] in Christ (the Messiah) he is a new creation (a new creature altogether); the old [previous moral and spiritual condition] has passed away. Behold, the fresh and new has come!

2 Corinthians 5:17

And all of us, as with unveiled face, [because we] continued to behold [in the Word of God] as in a mirror the glory of the Lord, are constantly being transfigured into His very own image in every increasing splendor and from one degree of glory to another.

2 Corinthians 3:18

No More Bumping Around in the Dark

Personally, I love seeing what I look like in the Word! It makes me feel good about myself. It gives me something to confess when I open my eyes first thing in the morning and I'm reminded of the mistakes I made yesterday. If I've been looking in the mirror of the Word, I don't have to pull the covers over my head and hide when I deal with accusations from the enemy or feelings of condemnation. I can get up with confidence and joy because of who I am in Christ! The more confidence we have as moms, the more confidence we will be able to instill in our children.

Another thing I love about looking in the Word is that it helps me see where I've been missing it. It sheds light on the dark areas of my life where I've been confused and I need wisdom. Areas where I've been bumping into things and making messes because I don't have enough light to see where I'm going wrong.

Some believers are afraid of that kind of light. They think being corrected by the Word is a negative thing. But it's not! It's like looking in a mirror and realizing you have a smudge of chocolate on your face or a piece of spinach between your teeth. You might feel a quick pang of embarrassment, but even so, you're glad you looked. Otherwise you might have gone through your whole day without correcting the problem.

I know what that's like. Before I started studying the Word, I lived for years without knowing what a mess I was. I thought everybody else was the problem. I thought my life was miserable because Dave needed to change...or my kids needed to change...or we needed a bigger home or more money. I needed the spiritual light of God's Word to see that the biggest change that needed to occur in my life was the change in *me*.

> *There is life, light, and life-changing power in the Word of God.*
>
>

Thank God for the Word! There is life, light, and life-changing power in the Word of God. It has completely revolutionized my life.

The same can be true for you. Not only can God's Word help you be a great mom, but it will tell you what you need to know to have victory in every area of life. That's why God said this in Joshua 1:8:

This Book of the Law shall not depart out of your mouth, but you shall meditate on it day and night, that you may observe and do according to all that is written in it. For then you shall make your way prosperous, and then you shall deal wisely and have good success.

When those words were first written, the only part of God's Word people could read was the *Book of the Law*, which consisted of the first five books of the Old Testament. Today we have the rest of the Old Testament and the New as well. If Joshua could deal wisely and have good success with the fraction of the Word he had, imagine what we can do with all that's available to us!

Be It Unto Me, Lord, According to Your Word

To see an example of a mother who was transformed by the miracle-working power of God's Word, all you have to do is read about Mary, the mother of Jesus. She was radically changed by looking into the mirror of the Word. She was just a normal, teenage girl living an ordinary life when the angel, Gabriel, appeared to her and said:

> ...Hail, O favored one [endued with grace]! The Lord is with you! Blessed (favored of God) are you before all other women...for you have found grace (free, spontaneous, absolute favor with and loving-kindness) with God. And listen! You will become pregnant and will give birth to a Son, and you shall call His name Jesus. He will be great (eminent) and will be called the Son of the Most High...."
>
> (Luke 1:28, 30-32)

That Word from God, wonderful as it was, didn't appear to match Mary's situation in any way. She wasn't anybody famous. The Bible doesn't indicate she'd had any spectacular experiences in her life that made her feel especially favored by God. What's more, she was a virgin. So she had every natural reason to say to Gabriel, "Sorry, Mr. Angel, but it looks like you came to the wrong address. I can't see how this Word from God could possibly apply to me."

But that's not how Mary responded. Instead of doubting God's Word, she believed it. She looked into His mirror, adjusted the way she saw herself and said, *Behold the handmaid of the Lord; be it unto me according to thy word* (Luke 1:38 KJV).

That's what you can say when you read what the Bible says about you!

When you read in 1 John 3:9, for instance, that *no one born (begotten) of God [deliberately, knowingly, and habitually] practices sin, for God's nature abides in him...* you can say, "That's the truth about me! God's nature abides in me. I don't have to yield to impatience or any other sin. I can be as patient and even tempered with my children as Jesus Himself is because His life is in me. Be it unto me, Lord, according to Your Word!"

"But Joyce," you might say, "I tried that and it didn't work. Two hours after I said it, the kids came screaming through the house with muddy feet and I blew up at them. I just can't change!"

Sure you can.

But to do so you need to remember that being transformed by the Word is a process. Jesus didn't say if you read a few Scriptures once or twice you'll be totally changed. He said, *If ye continue in my word, then are ye my disciples indeed; and ye shall know the truth, and the truth shall make you free* (John 8:31-32 KJV).

Think again about what happened to Mary. The promise of God was developing on the inside, yet, on the outside she didn't look any different for a while. It took time for the divine Seed within her to grow and develop into something the rest of the world could see.

As moms, we should understand this better than anyone else. We know firsthand what it's like to be pregnant and yet not be "showing." We've felt in our own bodies the invisible inward flutter of a newly conceived life. We didn't doubt our unborn baby's existence during those months it was still hidden inside us. We didn't get discouraged just because it hadn't yet made its appearance in the world.

No, we just trusted the process. We rejoiced and believed that as long as we provided the little life living in us with what it needed to thrive and grow, it would eventually become a kicking, smiling, beautiful baby we could actually hold in our arms.

That's the attitude you should take toward the seed of God's Word. It has His power built right into it. Just as a natural seed has the ability to reproduce the life that's in it, God's Word has the ability to reproduce in you His life, character, and nature. *For the Word that God speaks is alive and full of power [making it active, operative, energizing, and effective]* ... (Hebrews 4:12). It will empower you to be and do whatever it says about you.

So don't get discouraged just because you don't change overnight. Don't get angry with yourself and waste time feeling condemned every time you make a mistake. Just stick with the process! Keep drenching your spirit every day with the water of God's Word. Keep your eye on

God's mirror and say, "Be it unto me, Lord, according to Your Word."

Before long, what's being developed inside you will show up on the outside. More and more, you'll know and be able to do for your family exactly what Jesus would do.

CHAPTER 6

Take a Break . . . and Believe

Being a mom can be one of the most exhausting jobs on earth. Like most mothers, I figured that out as soon as my first baby was born. And with the arrival of each additional child, my revelation of this fact increased.

I can still vividly remember the time my daughter had colic as an infant and cried every night for weeks. I got so desperate for sleep that I called the doctor and gave him an ultimatum. "Either give me something to knock this child out or put me in a loony bin because *I can't take this anymore!*"

No doubt, you can relate.

Even if you haven't had a crib or a baby bottle in your house for years, as a mother you still face days when you're worn-out from everything you have to do. Days when you've given so much of yourself that you feel like you don't have anything left to give. Days when the demands of motherhood so drain your physical and emotional resources that you dream of going on vacation. Someplace far away. All by yourself. I have felt like running away from home a few times in my life, and you probably have felt the same way.

We all have these kinds of days—no mother is exempt from them. Whether we stay at home full-time or work a job, whether we're married or single, whether our bank accounts are fat or scrawny, we all get weary.

By definition, to be *weary* means to be "exhausted in strength or endurance, to have no vigor or freshness left, to have your inner resources depleted." It means you no longer have pleasure in what you do.

It also means you're in dangerous territory.

I've discovered—and you probably have too—that if I get too worn-out, I lose control of my emotions and get grouchy. I make bad decisions. I am tempted to overeat and overspend. I feel sorry for myself and tend not to resist temptation. It's no wonder the Bible says the devil seeks to "wear out" the saints (Daniel 7:25)! When we're worn-out, bummed-out, wrung-out, and barely able to drag ourselves around, we're easy prey for him. So if we're going to be the kind of moms we aspire to be, we can't afford to let ourselves get weary. We must make sure we're rested and refreshed each day.

Living on Vacation

I can almost hear you laughing right now. "Yeah, right, Joyce. I'll do that. Every time I get a little tired I'll just withdraw some of the money I won in the Publishers Clearing House Sweepstakes, leave the kids with Mary Poppins, and spend a few days in the Caribbean, swinging in a hammock, sipping coconut juice!"

If that's what you're thinking, I assure you, it's not what I'm suggesting. I realize you can't literally take a physical vacation every time you get weary. There's a good chance you can't even find time for a nap. But there is something you can do. You can take Jesus up on the offer He made in Matthew 11:28-29:

Come to Me, all you who labor and are heavy-laden and overburdened, and I will cause you to rest. [I will ease and relieve and refresh your souls.] Take My yoke upon you and learn of Me, for I am gentle (meek) and humble (lowly) in heart, and you will find rest (relief and ease and refreshment and recreation and blessed quiet) for your souls.

Think for a moment about the words Jesus used in that scripture. When you read them in this Amplified translation, they perfectly describe what every weary mom longs for: *rest, ease, refreshment, recreation, and blessed quiet.*

I don't know what comes to your mind when you hear those words, but they sound to me like a perfect vacation. And that's exactly what Jesus is talking about there. He's promising us a vacation—not for our bodies, but for our souls!

> *Imagine living every day with your soul on vacation.*

Imagine living every day with your soul on vacation. Imagine raising your kids, managing your household, taking care of business at the office, and doing everything else in your life, all in a place of supernatural rest. That's the way Jesus said we could live.

I'm not implying He promised us a trouble-free life. He didn't. What He said was we don't have to let the troubles of life exhaust us. We can connect with Him and let Him pull the load. Think of two oxen yoked together, one weak and the other infinitely strong. The weak one doesn't have to wear himself out. He doesn't have to worry that the work is too hard or the burden too heavy. All he has to do is stay in step and let the infinite strength of his yokefellow do for him everything that he can't do.

Hebrews 4 refers to this kind of living as entering "the rest" of God and says this is His will for us all. But sadly, few Christians consistently experience this rest. Although they take Jesus' yoke upon them at the moment of salvation, after they're saved they take it off again and wear themselves out trying to pull life's load on their own.

As mothers, we fall prey to this quite often. You know what I mean: We might be concerned that our child isn't popular enough, so we work ourselves to exhaustion putting together parties and inviting every kid in town. We might worry that our teenager will feel inferior if her clothes don't have designer labels, so we overcharge the credit cards, keeping her dressed to the hilt. We might be afraid that because we have to work outside the home our kids will feel deprived, so we give in to their every demand and refuse to tell them no. All the while, as we run ourselves to exhaustion, the Lord is saying:

Have you not known? Have you not heard? The everlasting God, the Lord, the Creator of the ends of the earth, does not faint or grow weary; there is no searching of His understanding. He gives power to the faint and weary, and to him who has no might He increases strength [causing it to multiply and making it to abound]. Even youths shall faint and be weary, and [selected] young men shall feebly stumble and fall exhausted; but those who wait for the Lord [who expect, look for, and hope in Him] shall change and

renew their strength and power; they shall lift their
wings and mount up [close to God] as eagles [mount
up to the sun]; they shall run and not be weary, they
shall walk and not faint or become tired.

Isaiah 40:28-31

It Is What It Is!

If you want some practical secrets about how to live with
your soul on vacation, you might want to make a study
of those verses. They don't just tell us we shouldn't get
weary. They tell us specifically what we can do to stay
supernaturally rested and refreshed.

Verse 28, for example, reminds us that there is no
searching of God's understanding. He knows infinitely
more than we do and He always will. We can leave it to
Him to solve all the problems we can't figure out and take
care of all the bad circumstances we're unable to change.

I don't mind admitting that was hard for me to learn
to do. I spent years asking, "Why, God, why?" or "When,
God, when?" I wasted enormous amounts of mental and
emotional energy struggling to fix people and situations
that were totally beyond my control. It was exhausting!
But I eventually realized it wasn't really the people and
circumstances that were draining me, it was the negative attitude with which I approached them. I often like

to ask, "Are your circumstances your problem, or is your attitude your problem?" My problem for many years was definitely my attitude.

That was the bad news. But then I discovered the good news: I can take a vacation from those negative attitudes anytime I choose. All I have to do is stop struggling and resenting the difficulties of life and decide to trust the Lord in the midst of them. All I have to do is take the attitude: *It is what it is*…and with God's help I can do what I need to do.

Don't misunderstand me; I'm not saying we should passively accept the works of the devil. I believe that God wants us to have a good life filled with peace and joy. He wants us to be blessed and have our needs met. The devil comes only to steal, kill, and destroy and we should resist him. God has not, however, redeemed us from every challenging situation and all difficult people. On the contrary, He often permits them in our lives, and He does so for only one purpose: to use them for our good (see Romans 8:28).

Once we understand this, we can live much more refreshing lives. Our souls can rest happily in a hammock of trust no matter what is happening around us— as long as we remain certain that Romans 8:28 is true: *All things work together and are [fitting into a plan] for good to and for those who love God and are called according to [His] design and purpose.*

"But I just can't figure out how God could ever bring good out of the problems I'm facing!" you might say. "I just wish He would tell me what He is doing."

I understand. I feel the same way sometimes. But I've found that God rarely shares with me exactly how He's going to work things out. He wants me to simply trust Him. He wants me to say—even when I don't understand or life seems unfair or I'm hurting so badly I can hardly stand it—"Lord, You know all things. You had this problem solved even before I had it. Although I don't know what You're going to do about it, I believe You love me, and I know You're going to do something good. So I'm not going to worry or be anxious. I'm going to rest in You."

Two Mighty Smart Boys

If you ever feel like you just *can't* relax and trust God, think about Sonya Carson. She's a mother who started out in life with more strikes against her than most of us can imagine. Born into a family of 24 children, she grew up in an atmosphere of poverty and abuse. She got married at 13 years old to a much older man, hoping for a better life. But instead, after having two sons, she found out her husband had another wife and family. Left with no other good option, Sonya divorced him and began raising her two boys alone.

A black woman in the 1960s, with only a third grade education, Sonya was totally unprepared for the hand life had dealt her. So the first few years after her divorce, she battled confusion and dangerous depression. Whenever it became too much for her, she sent 10-year-old Curtis and eight-year-old Ben to stay with friends or neighbors for a few weeks. She arranged for the boys to have so much fun while she was gone that they never guessed their mother secretly spent those weeks in a mental institution, trying to pull herself together and find a way to do what she had to do.

Thankfully, Sonya Carson was brave enough and smart enough to ask for help when she needed it—first from other people and ultimately from God. So it wasn't too long before she no longer needed to take those secret trips. In fact, she became so strong and so full of hope that nothing could shake her. Not the dwindling groceries in the pantry. Not the racial prejudice her boys faced at school. Not the fact that she sometimes worked three jobs at a time, spending long days caring for wealthy people's homes and families for minimum wages while her own children stayed home alone. Not even the failing grades young Ben brought home on his report card or his reputation as the worst student in his fifth grade class at Higgins Elementary School could shake her.

Sonya refused to allow any of those things to steal her

confidence in God. "Everything is going to be all right," she told Curtis and Ben. They believed it because she believed it so strongly herself. And when they talked to her about their own struggles, she always pointed them to the Source of her faith. "You just ask the Lord," she said, "and He will help you."

After Ben was grown, he wrote about one time in particular when his mother's trust in God helped chart the course for his life. He'd gone with her to one of the many church services they attended. The sermon had focused on medical missionaries who worked abroad and helped people live happier, healthier lives.

"That's what I want to do," I said to my mother as we walked home. "I want to be a doctor. Can I be a doctor, Mother?"

"Bennie," she said, "listen to me." We stopped walking and Mother stared into my eyes. Then laying her hands on my thin shoulders, she said, "If you ask the Lord for something and believe He will do it, then it'll happen."

"I believe I can be a doctor."

"Then, Bennie, you will be a doctor," she said matter-of-factly, and we started to walk on again.[1]

---

1. Ben Carson M.D. and Cecil Murphey, *Gifted Hands: The Ben Carson Story* (Zondervan).

Acting on her faith in God's ability to help her sons overcome the odds piled up against them, Sonya limited their TV watching and required them to read and write reports about two books a week. She marked the reports with her approval, never letting on that she was unable to read them. And even when naysaying teachers gave others reason to doubt her children's prospects for a bright future, Sonya continued to say, "I've got two smart boys. Two mighty smart boys!"

Not surprisingly, her words came to pass. Curtis went on to excel academically and became a mechanical engineer. Ben graduated from Yale, earned his medical degree at the University of Michigan, and became one of the world's most renowned neurosurgeons. He is best known for leading the surgical team that succeeded with one of the most groundbreaking operations ever attempted: the separation of Siamese twins joined at the head.

Lock Your Wings Upward

How could a mother who started out in such tragic circumstances come through in such triumph? There's only one explanation. She stopped asking, "Why, God, why?" and chose to believe that God would work all things together for her good. She stopped trying to pull the load of her circumstances by herself and yoked herself to Jesus. She decided to do what Isaiah 40 says and *wait on the Lord.*

When I say she waited on the Lord, clearly I'm not saying she sat and did nothing. That's not what waiting on the Lord means. It means looking to Him in faith with expectancy. It means believing His Word and resting on His faithfulness, even when the winds of adversity are churning around you.

Isaiah likens it to what an eagle does when he encounters a storm. Instead of wearing himself out by fighting against the winds, he locks his wings upward and lets the currents lift him higher and higher until he reaches an altitude where the storm is below him. And there he rests and rides it out in peace.

As mothers, we can do the same thing. When turbulence wearies us and threatens our family, we can lock our wings upward with the promises of God. Promises like...

- *Whatever you ask for in prayer, believe (trust and be confident) that it is granted to you, and you will [get it].*

Mark 11:24

- *All your . . . children shall be disciples [taught by the Lord and obedient to His will], and great shall be the peace and undisturbed composure of your children.*

  Isaiah 54:13

- *How joyful are those who fear the Lord and delight in obeying his commands. Their children will be successful everywhere; an entire generation of godly people will be blessed.*

  Psalm 112:1-2 NLT

- *I have never seen the godly abandoned, or their children begging for bread.*

  Psalm 37:25 NLT

- *In the reverent and worshipful fear of the Lord there is strong confidence, and His children shall always have a place of refuge.*

  Proverbs 14:26

- *The righteous man walks in his integrity; blessed (happy, fortunate, enviable) are his children after him.*

  Proverbs 20:7

• *Because God's your refuge, the High God your very own home, evil can't get close to you, harm can't get through the door.*

Psalm 91:9-10 MSG

• *God's love...is ever and always, eternally present to all who fear him, making everything right for them and their children.*

Psalm 103:17 MSG

I don't want to over-spiritualize here. There are times for every mom when we're physically weary and what we need most is natural or practical help. We need someone else to take out the trash, or wash the dishes, or sort the laundry. When you need that kind of help, ask for it. Let your children lend a hand. They might not do things the way you would, but it's better to have help that's imperfect than not to have help at all.

On the other hand, when it's not just your body but your soul that's worn-out, take a spiritual break. Spend a few minutes vacationing with Jesus. Grab your Bible and spend whatever minutes you can find accessing the Throne of Grace. Turn your spiritual wings upward with the promises of God and mount up to Him with wings like an eagle's.

Rest and ride high.

CHAPTER 7

No Fear Here!

*If you ask me what is the single most impor-
tant key to longevity, I'd say it's avoiding
worry...And if you didn't ask me, I'd still have
to say it.*

—George Burns

Of all the lies the devil has successfully sold Christian
mothers over the years, one of the most hazardous is
this: *All moms worry about their children.*

In the minds of many mothers, that lie is an undis-
puted fact. They accept worry not only as an inevita-
ble part of having children, but almost as a virtue. Read
a few articles and poems about motherhood and you'll
quickly see why. Many actually extol the idea that a
mother's love produces a constant state of anxiety. As
one poem, written in praise of the perpetually worried
mom, says:

"A mother's worry never ends. It just evolves and grows and starts again."

Please do not believe this. It is not in the Bible. On the contrary, the Bible tells us 365 times to *"Fear not!"* That's one time for every day of the year. And nowhere in the Scripture is a footnote added that says: *In the case of mothers, this command does not apply.*

As moms, however, we often act as if such footnotes abound. We think, *Well, God knows that as parents we care so much about our children we can't help but be afraid for them. So when we worry, He understands.*

Jesus never tells us to worry, nor does He approve of it. One parent who can confirm that is Jairus. He came to Jesus for help when he was in the midst of one of the worst crises any parent can face: His little daughter was dying. Her condition was so critical and he was so desperate for help that he threw himself on the ground at Jesus' feet and begged Him earnestly, saying, *"...Come and lay Your hands on her, that she may be healed, and she will live"* (Mark 5:23, NKJV).

If you've read the story, you know what happened next. Jesus responded to Jairus' words of faith and headed right away toward his house. But before getting there, they encountered an unexpected interruption. A woman who'd been sick for 12 years fought her way through the crowd that was trailing after Jesus, touched the hem of His garment, and was instantly healed.

And Jesus, recognizing in Himself that the power proceeding from Him had gone forth, turned around immediately in the crowd and said, Who touched My clothes? And the disciples kept saying to Him, You see the crowd pressing hard around You from all sides, and You ask, Who touched Me? Still He kept looking around to see her who had done it. But the woman, knowing what had been done for her...fell down before Him and told Him the whole truth (vv. 30-33).

The Bible doesn't say how long it took this woman to tell Jesus "the whole truth." But if she was like most women I know, it took her quite a while to describe 12 years of sickness. Meanwhile, Jairus was standing there thinking, *Lady, my daughter is at the very point of death! Every second counts! Please...pleeeease...hurry up!*

In spite of the delay, Jairus apparently managed to hold on to his faith...until things got worse. Some people came running from his house and said to him, *Your daughter has died. Why bother and distress the Teacher any further?* (v. 35). Talk about having an excuse to worry—Jairus really did! He'd just gotten the worst news imaginable. Yet Jesus, overhearing the report, said in no uncertain terms...

Do not be seized with alarm and struck with fear; only keep on believing (v. 36).

Why did Jesus give those seemingly unrealistic instructions to Jairus? Why was it so important to Him that Jairus refuse to fear at that crucial moment in his life?

Because Jesus knew what most people (even most Christians) don't: That just as faith connects us to God's plan for our lives, fear can disconnect us from it and connect us to the devil's plan.

Job 3:25 says, *For the thing which I greatly fear comes upon me, and that of which I am afraid befalls me.* Jesus didn't want that to happen to Jairus. He didn't want the door Jairus' faith had opened for Him to work a miracle in his daughter's life to be slammed shut by fear.

That's the turn the story was about to take. But thanks to the faith of Jairus and the power of Jesus, things didn't go that way! Jairus' daughter was healed because her father chose faith over fear. He proved that even when parental emotions are screaming, we can choose to obey Jesus. We can keep the door open to God's best for our children by choosing to believe and fear not!

Don't Drink the Poison

Before you get too alarmed about the power of fear (and add fear to your list of things to worry about) let me assure you, the Bible doesn't teach that every little fear you've ever had about your kids is going to become a reality. That's not true. Although the devil does work through fear much like God works through faith, the devil isn't even nearly as powerful as God is. That's why he was only able to bring upon Job the things that he "greatly" feared.

Though small worries aren't great fears, those small worries open the door to fear in your life. You probably already know this from experience, but let me just remind you of some of the effects worry can have on your life. It can:

- Keep you fretting about tomorrow and steal your joy today.
- Drain you of your enthusiasm for life and darken your days with...*anxious thoughts and forebodings* (Proverbs 15:15).
- Waste your time. (Has worry ever helped you in any way? No!) *Who of you by worrying and being anxious can add one unit of measure (cubit) to his stature or to the span of his life?* (Matthew 6:27).
- Make you sick. (Doctors tell us that at least 51 diseases can be directly connected to worry and stress!)
- Torture you mentally and emotionally. (Worry can actually be defined as tormenting one's self with disturbing thoughts!)

On top of all that, worrying is disobeying God's command. To do it is a sin. So obviously, to be a confident mom, you must break the worry habit!

You might be thinking, *But some of the concerns I have about my children are very real. I can't just ignore them.*

Of course, you can't. But what you can do is follow the instructions in Philippians 4:6-8:

> *Do not fret or have any anxiety about anything, but in every circumstance and in everything, by prayer and petition (definite requests), with thanksgiving, continue to make your wants known to God. And God's peace...which transcends all understanding shall garrison and mount guard over your hearts and minds in Christ Jesus. For the rest...whatever is true... whatever is kind and winsome and gracious, if there is any virtue and excellence, if there is anything worthy of praise, think on and weigh and take account of these things [fix your minds on them].*

Did you notice that last phrase? It says we can fix our mind on God's Word instead of our worries. We can mentally rehearse and continually confess the promises of God over our lives and the lives of our children. That's what meditation is! People often tell me they don't know how to meditate on the Word. But they're mistaken. We all know how to meditate on God's Word because we've done it in reverse! We've listened to worry and anxiety and meditated on them until we believed them, spoke them, and acted on them.

I did that for years without even realizing it. Before I started studying the Word, it never occurred to me that the enemy might be behind my negative thoughts. I assumed I came up with them myself so I'd just think about whatever fell into my mind. If it occurred to me that I should be worried about something, I'd just think, *Yeah, that situation could turn out really badly! Why, it could ruin my whole life!* And off I'd go on a mental tangent. I didn't realize back then that the devil had the power of suggestion, that he actually flashes thoughts across our minds so that we'll accept them and meditate on them.

But eventually, by studying the Word, I got a clue! I realized that fearful thoughts are like the devil's poison. He's always going to be offering it to us. But just because he offers it doesn't mean we have to drink it. Instead we can do what 2 Timothy 2:23 tells us to do: *Refuse (shut your mind against, have nothing to do with) trifling (ill-informed, unedifying, stupid) controversies....* We can say,

"No! I will not worry. I will choose to meditate on God's Word and believe His promises."

Actually, let me put that a little stronger. Not only *can* we say such things, we *should* say them. Why? Because it's impossible to think one thing and say another at the same time. Therefore the best way there is to get rid of worried thoughts is by opening our mouths and speaking the Word.

"But I'll feel stupid talking to myself!"

Yes, at first you probably will. I know I did. But I decided I'd rather *feel* a bit foolish than live in defeat and despair. So I let go of my pride and began to speak God's Word out loud over my life multiple times a day.

Sometimes I've even had to talk myself out of worrying while I was getting ready to go out and preach about—of all things—not worrying! I remember one time in particular when something was really bothering me. And for whatever reason, I started getting anxious and upset, and the second I realized it, I opened my mouth and acted on Philippians 4:6. I said, "Lord, there is nothing at all I can do about this situation. So I put it in Your hands right now. I ask You to take care of it, and I thank You in advance for doing so." Then I sang praise songs to the Lord until I could step out on the platform without worry.

Do It by Faith and Your Feelings
Will Catch Up

On ordinary days, most of the fears moms have to conquer are relatively minor. They involve things like potty training, pouting, poor grades in school, and puberty. When we do have to deal with major concerns, however, it's important for us to remember that the same declarations of faith we use to defeat the smallest of worries can be used to chop the heads off giant-sized worries as well.

David proved it in his battle with Goliath.

That battle, although most people don't realize it, was primarily a war of words. Goliath started it by saying things meant to terrify the entire Israelite army and ultimately David. Things like, "Come to me, and I will give your flesh to the birds of the air and the beasts of the field" (1 Samuel 17:44). (Doesn't that sound intimidating?)

Goliath's words made everybody else shake in their sandals, but David refused to be afraid. Instead he raised his voice and fought back:

You come to me with a sword, a spear, and a javelin, but I come to you in the name of the Lord of hosts, the God of the ranks of Israel, Whom you have defied. This day the Lord will deliver you into my hand, and I will smite you and cut off your head. And I will give the corpses of the army of the Philistines this day to the birds of the air and the wild beasts of the earth, that all the earth may know that there is a God in Israel. And all this assembly shall know that the Lord saves not with sword and spear; for the battle is the Lord's, and He will give you into our hands (1 Samuel 17:45-47).

The devil hates that kind of talk. Whether it's coming from an Israelite shepherd boy or from a Christian mother, he hates it when believers start verbally swinging the "sword of the Spirit," which is the Word of God. And, considering how Goliath ended up, it's easy to see why.

Even one faith-filled sentence can completely defeat one of the devil's evil plans.

One mom I know of demonstrated that in a dramatic way. Some years ago on Christmas Day, her 11-year-old daughter came down with a life-threatening strain of meningitis. She and her husband rushed the girl to the hospital, and there, doctors informed them that an epidemic of the disease had broken out. Several children had already died. "Your daughter's case is the worst we've seen yet," the doctor said.

For this mom, it was her Jairus moment. But she was ready.

Having grown up as a minister's daughter in a strong

family of faith, she knew healing had been purchased for her and her children through God's plan of redemption. She knew and believed that *with the stripes [that wounded] Him we are healed and made whole* (Isaiah 53:5). So when her sister—who was another Bible-believing mama—walked through the emergency room doors, she took the opportunity to make her declaration. She gritted her teeth against the emotions that assaulted her, looked her sister in the eyes, and said:

"I...WILL...*NOT*...FEAR!"

Notice, she didn't say that she didn't *feel* afraid. In fact, she didn't say anything at all about how she felt because emotions don't have to dictate our decisions.

> *Just because we feel afraid doesn't mean we have to be afraid.*

Just because we feel afraid doesn't mean we have to be afraid. We can take our stand by faith on God's Word and reject fear by refusing to speak it or act on it. If we do that, our feelings will eventually catch up with our decision.

I don't know how long it took this mother's feelings to catch up. Maybe it happened within the next few minutes. Or maybe she had to override emotions all during the hours that she and her family continued to pray about the situation and speak God's Word. But one way or the other, I'm sure her emotions felt just fine the next day because her daughter, who'd been unable to speak for hours, sat up in bed and shouted to her grandfather, who was standing by her hospital bed, declaring God's Word:

"Paw-paw, I'm healed in the Name of Jesus!"

Isn't that amazing? That little girl, as young and sick as she was, perfectly followed her mother's example! Not the example that was set a few hours before in the waiting area of the emergency room—the daughter hadn't been there to witness that—but the example she'd seen all her life as she'd watched her mother choose faith instead of fear.

I've already said this, but I'll say it again: Whatever you do consistently is what your children will learn to do.

If you yield constantly to worry, they'll be prone to torment themselves with disturbing thoughts.

> *Whatever you do consistently is what your children will learn to do.*

If you choose to believe and speak God's Word and set a fearless example, they'll be likely to enjoy life, swing the sword of God's Word, and win battles.

That's what happened in this situation. The mother's first words of faith worked like the first stone that took down Goliath. The daughter's words became the sword that severed his head. Once they were spoken, she immediately began to get better. The victory was won.

Yes, You Can!

If you've been a hard-core worrier for years, you may be wondering right now if you'll ever be able to stop. You may not be confident that it's even possible for you to say, like the mom in the story did, "I will not fear!"

But I assure you, it is.

How can I be so certain? Because God would never tell us to do something without giving us the ability to do it. So the very fact that, in the Bible, He instructed us not to fear and not to worry proves He has given us the power to do it.

What's more, 1 John 4:17 tells us that as Jesus is, *so are we in this world*. That means we don't have to wait until we die and go to Heaven to be like Him. We can live like Him right here and now. Let me ask you: Do you think Jesus is afraid right now? Do you think He is wringing His hands and fretting over how dark and dangerous this world has become? Do you think He's worrying about whether or not He can handle it?

Of course not!

Jesus isn't worried; He is full of peace. And if He has peace, we can have peace. As He said in John 14:27:

Peace I leave with you; My [own] peace I now give and bequeath to you. Not as the world gives do I give to you. Do not let your hearts be troubled, neither let them be afraid. [Stop allowing yourselves to be agitated and disturbed; and do not permit yourselves to be fearful and intimidated and cowardly and unsettled.]

The very peace of Jesus Himself is available to you 24/7. So make the choice that Jairus made and remember to *give all your worries and cares to God, for he cares about you* (1 Peter 5:7 NLT).

Fear not. Only believe.

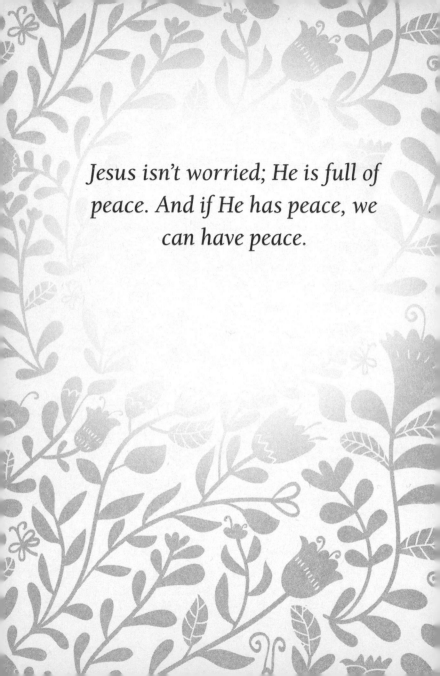

Jesus isn't worried; He is full of peace. And if He has peace, we can have peace.

CHAPTER 8

Can Somebody Please Help Me?

Raising a family would be so much easier if God had given moms a one-size-fits-all strategy for raising children. It would make motherhood much more convenient. We'd never have to second-guess our parenting choices. We'd never lie awake in bed at night wondering if we're too strict or too lenient. We'd never have moments when we feel like tearing our hair out because we *just can't understand this child!*

Instead, we could simply buy a handbook, follow the instructions step-by-step and—presto!—magically everything would turn out exactly the way God intended.

Oh, how simple that would be!

Unfortunately, that is not the way things actually work. Although God has given mothers general guidelines and unchanging scriptural truths that can point us all in the right direction, every child is one-of-a-kind and needs specialized care and training. Each has a unique combination of personality, talents, and tendencies. Each must navigate a different set of circumstances. And each has their own God-ordained calling. As mothers, we must take all these things into account and parent every one of our children in a way that helps them become the person God created them to be.

Talk about *Mission Impossible*! It's no wonder that so many mothers walk around with this cry rising up from their hearts: *Can somebody please help me?*

That's a question moms have been asking in one way or another for thousands of years. And it's a question God has answered. Throughout the Bible, He demonstrated again and again that when mothers need a unique plan for a unique child in a unique situation, God can help like nobody else can.

> *Throughout the Bible, He demonstrated again and again that when mothers need a unique plan for a unique child in a unique situation, God can help like nobody else can.*

Take, for instance, the child-development plan He came up with for Jochebed. She was Moses' mother and, as you probably remember, she faced an extremely unusual and distressing situation. Her baby boy was divinely destined for greatness. He was appointed by God to be a nation-deliverer and a world changer. But as a Hebrew male in Egypt, he was born facing a death sentence. According to Pharaoh's edict, anybody who saw him was legally obligated to kill him on the spot!

Jochebed's mission was to keep her son alive...and there was nobody on earth who could tell her how to do it. No friends she could ask. No books she could read. No hotlines she could call.

So what did she do?

For the first three months of her baby's life, she hid him from the world and pondered her predicament. As a descendent of Abraham, she must have also looked to God for help. As she did, a plan began to emerge in her mind—a plan that had never been implemented before and never would again.

> ...She got a basket made of papyrus reeds and water-proofed it with tar and pitch. She put the baby in the basket and laid it among the reeds along the bank of the Nile River. The baby's sister then stood at a distance, watching to see what would happen to him (Exodus 2:3-4 NLT).

For most of us, the thought of baby Moses floating around in a basket brings back memories of Sunday school lessons and cloth cutouts on felt boards. But for

Jochebed, this wasn't a Bible story. This was her life. This was her baby! And she wasn't just sailing him across a swimming pool on a rubber raft with floaties on his arms. She was launching him into the dangers of the Nile. She was setting her helpless infant adrift, alone, in waters where hippos wallowed on one bank and Pharaoh's daughter bathed on the other, with no idea which of the two might prove to be more deadly.

Can you imagine Jochebed trying to explain this survival strategy to the other mothers in the neighborhood? It would have sounded absurd. "You can't be serious!" they would have gasped. "Why didn't you just let the poor little fellow die quickly at the hands of Pharaoh's soldiers? Wouldn't that be kinder than putting him out there to drown or to be eaten by a wild animal?"

Thankfully, Jochebed never had to face such consequences. Her plan—because it was God's plan—succeeded before anyone found out about it. Not only did her little boy survive, he got the opportunity to grow up in Pharaoh's courts. Educated and surrounded by Egypt's best, he got all the training he needed to fulfill the future God had in mind for him.

Best of all, at least from Jochebed's perspective, was this: She got to go with him to the palace and be his nanny…and *Mission Impossible* became *Mission Accomplished*!

The Holy Spirit: Your Greatest Helper

"But that was *Moses'* mother!" you might say. "She's a scriptural celebrity. I'm just an ordinary mom. I can't expect God to help me the way He helped her."

Why not? Jesus said the least of us who've been born again into God's kingdom are greater than the greatest Old Testament prophet that ever lived. (See Matthew 11:11.) So anything God would do for Jochebed or any other mom in the Bible, He will do for you.

He may also do it differently than He did for mothers in the Old Testament. Because you're a born-again, New Testament believer, you don't need an angel to appear from Heaven and bring you a message. You don't need to hear a voice booming instructions at you out of the sky. You don't need to see handwriting on the wall. You have the Holy Spirit living inside of you to lead you and speak to you all the time.

The Holy Spirit is the greatest Helper that you, as a mom, could ever have!

He not only understands your children's personalities and giftings, He knows what God has ordained them to be and do. He knows what kind of encouragement they need and what style of discipline they'll respond to. He can alert you when they're headed for trouble and show you how to deal with it. When you make mistakes, He can show you how to make things right again. The Spirit of God will tell you everything you need to know. He'll give you divine wisdom for every situation you face, 24 hours a day, seven days a week.

We know this is true because Jesus told us it was. Jesus promised that after He was crucified and resurrected, the Holy Spirit would come and remain with us forever. *I will not leave you as orphans, [comfortless, desolate, bereaved, forlorn, helpless],* He said. *But the Comforter (Counselor, Helper, Intercessor, Advocate, Strengthener, Standby), the Holy Spirit, Whom the Father will send in My name [in My place to represent Me and act on My behalf], He will:*

- Teach you all things.
- Cause you to recall…everything I have told you.
- Be in close fellowship with you.
- Guide you into all the Truth (the whole, full Truth) (John 14:18, 26; 16:7, 13).

Clearly, if Jesus said the Holy Spirit will do all those things for us, He will!

Then why does it often seem like so many believers are floundering around on their own? Why don't we benefit more from the ministry of this Helper we've been given?

Usually it's because we run to other people for answers instead of to God. It's a strange thing to do, given that other people know very little and the Lord knows everything, but we tend to do it anyway for one primary reason: We're not confident we can truly hear the Lord's voice and discern His wisdom and direction, or in some cases we don't even know that doing so is an option.

This is a major problem for many Christians! But if you're among those who struggle with it, there is a solution. You can strengthen your confidence in your divine connection with the Holy Spirit by focusing on what the Bible says in verses like these:

> Jesus said, *The sheep that are My own hear and are listening to My voice; and I know them, and they follow me* (John 10:27). Therefore I can discern the leading of the Lord. I can follow Him!

> *The Spirit of Truth, Whom the world cannot receive (welcome, take to its heart), because it does not see Him or know and recognize Him. But you know and recognize Him, for He lives with you [constantly] and will be in you* (John 14:17). I can know and recognize the Spirit of God because He lives in me!

> *For all who are led by the Spirit of God are children of God* (Romans 8:14 NLT). I am a child of God, therefore I am led by the Spirit!

For the Spirit teaches you everything you need to know, and what he teaches is true—it is not a lie. So just as he has taught you, remain in fellowship with Christ (1 John 2:27 NLT). The Holy Spirit will teach me what is true!

As you meditate on such scriptures and make confessions of faith, you'll grow in your relationship with your divine Helper. You'll develop more faith in the truth that as a believer, you are perfectly equipped with everything you need to hear from Him, and then respond in obedience to His instructions.

Don't Forget to Ask

Another key to tapping into the wisdom that God has to offer you and your children is this: Remember to ask Him for it, expecting Him to answer. Sometimes in the busyness of life, we forget to do this. Yet it's so important, the Bible repeatedly encourages us:

If any of you is deficient in wisdom, let him ask of the giving God [Who gives] to everyone liberally and ungrudgingly, without reproaching or faultfinding, and it will be given him. Only it must be in faith that he asks with no wavering (no hesitating, no doubt-

ing). For the one who wavers (hesitates, doubts) is like the billowing surge out at sea that is blown hither and thither and tossed by the wind.

James 1:5-6

Ask and keep on asking and it shall be given you; seek and keep on seeking and you shall find; knock and keep on knocking and the door shall be opened to you. If you... give good gifts [gifts that are to their advantage] to your children, how much more will your heavenly Father give the Holy Spirit to those who ask and continue to ask Him!

Luke 11:9, 13

If you cry out for insight and raise your voice for understanding, if you seek [Wisdom] as for silver and search for skillful and godly Wisdom as for hidden treasures, then you will understand the reverent and worshipful fear of the Lord and find the knowledge of [our omniscient] God.

Proverbs 2:3-5

How simple is that? Just ask for wisdom and trust God to give it to you! If you don't hear from Him the split-second you pray, keep believing Him and looking inside your heart to see what God is showing you. The answer will always come.

Of course, once it does, to enjoy its benefits you have to "embrace" it (see Proverbs 4:8). That's not always easy to do because sometimes God's wisdom requires you to step out of your comfort zone. Although you'll probably never have to venture as far outside of it as Jochebed did, as a Christian mom, being led by the Holy Spirit may challenge you to make choices for your children that others may not understand or perhaps might even criticize.

I remember one time in particular when that was true for me. It was back when our son, Danny, was in grade school. Pretty much from the time he was born, I'd planned for him to attend a Christian school. My daughter had gone to a certain Christian school for years and had done just fine. So when Danny was old enough, he started going there too. That's what I assumed would be best.

He ended up in a class where some of the students began to pick on him. His schoolwork suffered, and he started falling behind academically. The teachers kept promoting him from grade to grade anyway, but he was struggling so much that we knew we had to make a change. We even hired tutors to help him and did everything else we could think of, but nothing worked. The system at that particular school was quite strict, and his personality was very resistant to extensive rules and regulations. He was constantly getting into trouble, and that only served to make him dread even the thought of going to school.

As you can imagine, I really sought God for wisdom about the situation. After praying about it for a while, He gave me the answer. It was not the one I wanted to hear. He led Dave and me to transfer our son to the public school across the street from our house.

This would not have been my choice, but it was what God was leading us to do. I can just tell you that it was not *my* plan, so it took me a while to embrace this idea for a couple of reasons. First, it was contrary to my own opinions. Second, I was concerned about what my pastor and other people might think of me. Finally, though, I decided to obey the Holy Spirit's leading, and I enrolled Danny in public school. The school had some refreshing ideas about education that included not expecting all children to learn the exact same way, and this was exactly what was needed in our situation. Our son was and is quite brilliant, but he learned much quicker from a "hands-on" approach rather than merely through books.

The first day I took him there, I cried. I felt like I was somehow failing as a Christian mother. But amazingly enough, he flourished there. He made good grades. Although he still had some struggles, things were at least 75 percent better. Eventually we did return to tutoring at home because it allowed him to travel with us, but my point is that there are times when the Holy Spirit will lead us to do things that we would not ordinarily choose. It might encourage some of you moms who are struggling with a child in school to know that Dan is now CEO of Joyce Meyer Ministries and does an amazingly great job. Trust me when I tell you that even a child who struggles with organized education can still accomplish great things in life.

I now realize that in the area of how to educate our children—as in every other area of life—the best thing we as moms can do is seek the wisdom of the Holy Spirit and obey it. It might be different than what we thought, and it might be different from what other people are doing, but God has a plan and we can trust His guidance. After all, He knows far more about our children than we ever will.

He is truly a mother's greatest Helper!

The Holy Spirit is the greatest Helper that you, as a mom, could ever have!

CHAPTER 9

Accentuate the Positive

A frustrated mother was once asked whether or not she'd have children if she had it to do over again. "Yes," she replied. "But not the same ones."

I think there are moments when almost any mom would be tempted to give that answer. There are times when our children—as wonderful as they are—can test our patience. They do it in any number of ways, of course, but I'd have to say that when my kids were younger, it wasn't their natural weaknesses I found most trying, it was negative attitudes.

There are few things more aggravating to us as parents than complaining, ungrateful kids. After all, we pour our lives into them. We love them, pray for them, feed them, clothe them, school them, and do everything else we possibly can to bless them. All we really want in return is for them to be happy and grateful. So when they grumble about everything that's wrong with their lives and everything they don't have, it grieves our heart. As parents, we want to be appreciated!!!! We don't like it when our children have negative attitudes, but is it possible that they inherited them from us? Is it possible that we are seeing a mirror image of our own behavior? As parents we should strive to be good examples to our children in all things, and that certainly includes having a good, positive and grateful attitude. We cannot expect our children not to complain if they hear us complaining.

It saddens God when we, as His children, ignore all the blessings He has given us and focus instead on the things we're unhappy about. It grieves His heart when we complain about the battles we're facing in life instead of celebrating all the victories that, by God's grace and goodness, we've already won! That's why in the Bible He said this:

> *Be happy [in your faith] and rejoice and be glad-hearted continually (always); be unceasing in prayer [praying perseveringly]; thank [God] in everything [no matter what the circumstances may be, be thankful and give thanks], for this is the will of God for you [who are] in Christ Jesus...Do not quench (suppress or subdue) the Holy Spirit.*
>
> 1 Thessalonians 5:16-19

Those are very clear and simple instructions. But you know as well as I do, we're often inclined to argue about them. "Well, I know I shouldn't be so irritable but I just have a lot to deal with," we say. "My bank balance is low and my car needs new tires. My kids have allergies and need braces. My boss is a jerk, my husband spends every weekend watching football on TV, and my neighbor has a barking dog that won't shut up. Surely God doesn't expect me to be glad-hearted and thankful in the middle of all that!"

Yes, actually He does. Because while all those things may be true, so is this: By His grace we've been saved from our sins, we have hope in all things, and we're headed for an eternity in Heaven. We have a Bible full of promises that can help us conquer every challenge we're facing. We have a heavenly Father who loves us without limits and whose mercy has no end.

Because of His goodness, we have air to breathe, a heart that beats, and a family to love. And without Him, we wouldn't have anything: not a bank account of any size, a car (with or without tires), a child or children, a job, a husband, or modern appliances. We wouldn't even have ears to hear a barking dog.

I take care of my mom and aunt who are both now in a nursing home. Their health has diminished and their mobility is quite limited. They either sit in a chair or lie in bed most of the time. A short while ago I was visiting my aunt and she said, "Honey, I would love to have a few peaches from the store." Her simple request reminded me of how we often take little things in life for granted. I gladly went to the store and got her three big peaches and was thankful that I could get peaches, or anything else I wanted to eat, anytime I wanted to. That incident reminded me of how I enjoy getting a coffee from Starbucks or a homegrown tomato from the farmers' market, and I was extra thankful that day.

I would like to say that is my attitude every day, but there are many days when it is just easier to drift toward the negative. If I don't spend time with the Lord every day and purposely set myself to obey Him and yield to the fruit of the Spirit, I can start seeing what is wrong with life instead of what is right. So does everybody else. Simply because of the nature of the flesh, it takes effort for human beings to be positive and thankful.

Being grouchy, however, comes very easily.

The "ites" Are Not the Problem

The Israelites that God delivered out of Egypt demonstrated this in a major way. They were famous for being world-champion gripers. Yet they had more reasons to rejoice than any other group of people in the entire Old

Testament. God did absolutely amazing things for them! He brought the greatest nation in the world to its knees in order to set them free from a grueling life of slavery. He healed them all. He prospered them with silver and gold. He saved them from Pharaoh's army, split the Red Sea, and led them through on dry ground.

As if that wasn't enough, He led them through the wilderness with the cloud and fire of His presence by day and by night. He fed them from Heaven when they were hungry. And when they got thirsty, He poured water out of a rock.

He also promised to bring them into a land of milk and honey where they'd prosper and be blessed. But most of them never got to live there because they did the same thing we often do today. They . . . *grumbled and deplored their hardships, which was evil in the ears of the Lord, and when the Lord heard it, His anger was kindled; and the fire of the Lord burned among them and devoured those in the outlying parts of the camp* (Numbers 11:1).

Thank God we live under the New Covenant and not under the Old! We don't have to worry about God burning down our house because we grumble. But that doesn't mean we can do it without any consequences. Ingratitude and complaining is a sin today just like it was back then. When we engage in it, we open the door to the devil and, before we know it, he has our home in a mess. He's got our husband irritated and snappy. He's got the kids fighting and complaining. All because we acted like Mrs. Grouch and invited him in. Always remember that gratitude keeps the devil away, but when we complain, he is here to stay!

You'd think after doing that once or twice, we'd learn our lesson. But we usually don't. Neither did the Israelites.

Just a couple of chapters after they got scorched by the fire of the Lord, they were back at it again. This time they were upset because they'd heard there were enemies living in their Promised Land. I don't know why that news caught them so off guard. The Lord had told them they'd have to drive out the Canaanites, the Hittites, the Amorites, and a lot of other "ites." He also assured them time and again that He'd empower them to win every battle. But somehow they forgot. So...

All the congregation cried out with a loud voice, and [they] wept that night. All the Israelites grumbled and deplored their situation, accusing Moses and Aaron, to whom the whole congregation said, Would that we had died...in this wilderness! Why does the Lord bring us to this land to fall by the sword? Our wives and little ones will be a prey. Is it not better for us to return to Egypt?

Numbers 14:1-3

As a result of their complaining, that generation of Israelites never entered the Promised Land; instead, their grumbling and complaining about the "ites" they would face kept them short of God's best for their lives.

It is easy to see how important a thankful attitude is when we consider how many thousands of times the Bible instructs us to be thankful, to give praise and to worship God. It is not just a nice thing to do, but that kind of positive, grateful attitude is very powerful.

Many Christians today wind up doing much the same thing the Israelites did. They receive Jesus as Savior, but they stop short of their Promised Land. Instead of enjoying all the blessings God has provided for them, they spend years wandering around in the wilderness complaining about their "ites."

You know what I'm talking about. We all have our "ites." We have the insensitive-husband-ites, the oh-my-aching-back-ites, the bad-economy-ites, the child-that's-driving-me-crazy-ites. But for us, and just like the people of Israel, the "ites" aren't really the problem. They aren't keeping us out of our Promised Land.

What keeps us out sometimes could simply be a bad attitude! I can confirm this from personal experience because I used to be the queen of bad attitudes. I was raised in such a negative environment that I could find something wrong with everything. I saw "ites" everywhere I looked.

When I married Dave, I decided he was the biggest one of all. So I spent years grumbling, complaining, and telling God that Dave was making me miserable.

Eventually, God got through to me. "Joyce, Dave is not the problem," He said. "The problem is *you*." I seriously needed an attitude change, and thankfully God helped me before all my children were grown and I still had time to influence them in a positive way.

The Day the Pie Fell

The revelation that I had a bad attitude came as a shock, and initially, I wasn't thrilled about it. So I can sympathize if you're feeling less than thrilled right now yourself. This kind of information is hard on our flesh. It's tough to give up the blame game and face the fact that we're responsible for our own attitudes. But if we do it, it will open the door to wonderful changes in our lives— especially for those of us who are moms.

You see, as mothers, our negative attitudes not only grieve the Spirit of God, they grieve our family too. As somebody once said, "The mother is like the thermostat of the home. She determines the climate." When we're negative and ungrateful, our children tend to be that way too. When we're positive and thankful, they reflect those attitudes. Over time, the attitudes our children consistently see in us are likely to take root in them and become their own.

That's what happened to Debbie Morris. A minister's wife, she is well known among friends and congregation members for her cheerful, gracious temperament. Like all of us, she's had to work at it by studying the Bible and growing in the Lord, but she also gives her mom some of the credit.

She tells about one particular incident in her childhood when her mother's positive attitude made a permanent impression. It was the day the pie fell. "I'll never forget it," Debbie says.

> [Mom had] spent the whole day cleaning house from top to bottom because guests were coming. Everything was ready except for the pie. One of those cream cheese affairs in a graham cracker crust with cherry topping, it was assembled but still needed to chill for a while. As my sister and I watched, mouths watering, my mom lifted the pie from the counter to put it in the refrigerator when tragedy struck. The pie took a tumble and went splat on her sparkling clean kitchen floor.
>
> For one awful moment, all three of us stared at it in shock. Then, with great grace, my mom reached into the silverware drawer and took out three spoons. "Let's eat!" she said with a grin. So we all sat

down and had a pie party on the floor...It's a memory I'll always cherish. And it happened because my mother chose to be gracious, not grouchy.[1]

A good attitude doesn't come from having the best of everything in life; it comes from making the best of everything in life! Debbie's mom proved it that day. She recognized that her attitude belonged to her and she alone got to choose what she was going to do with it. So she chose wisely—not just for her own sake, but for her children's. In doing so, she set a good example for us all to follow.

> A good attitude doesn't come from having the best of everything in life; it comes from making the best of everything in life!

Please hear my heart on this; I don't mean to minimize the problems you might be facing right now. I realize they may be much bigger and more serious than an overturned pie. But the principle still remains the same. In any situation, you can choose to be positive. You can decide to count your blessings and remember all the things God has done for you.

---

1. Debbie Morris, *The Blessed Woman* (Southlake, TX; Gateway Create, 2012), 90-91.

I've read about Jewish people in German concentration camps during World War II who did this! They decided that the one thing their enemy couldn't steal from them was their good attitude. So, no matter what happened, they refused to let go of it. Even in the midst of the most unthinkable tragedy, they found something to be grateful for.

Oh, how wonderful it is that God gave us the ability to look at negative things from a positive perspective! It enables us to turn the trials of life into opportunities to build our character and experience God's power in the most profound way. It takes what we thought was our worst enemy and makes it our best friend. It allows us to see for ourselves why the Bible says:

All things work together and are [fitting into a plan] for good to and for those who love God and are called according to [His] design and purpose.

Romans 8:28

When troubles come your way, consider it an opportunity for great joy. For...when your faith is tested, your endurance has a chance to grow. So let it grow, for when your endurance is fully developed, you will be perfect and complete, needing nothing.

James 1:2-4 NLT

[Others] thought evil against me, but God meant it for good....

Genesis 50:20

A few years ago, I was preparing to preach a message in which I was going to share my full testimony. As I sat down to make some notes about the details of the abuse I suffered in my past, I was awed all over again by what God has done for me. He's taken what the devil meant for my destruction, delivered me from it, and used it to spur me on in ministry. Today, the pain I experienced in my past has become one of the major reasons I preach with such passion.

Truly, God can bring good out of anything! That's the reason we can be glad-hearted continually and thank Him in everything no matter what the circumstances may be.

I realize, it's not easy to do sometimes. When

Truly, God can bring good out of anything!

things happen that seem unfair, or difficult times last longer than you expected, you'll always be tempted to complain. But when you face that temptation, remember this: Complaining never helps; it just makes bad situations worse and hinders the work of God in your life.

Being glad-hearted and thankful, on the other hand, does just the opposite. It keeps your focus on the Lord, and it opens the door for your victory. It not only makes your family happier, it keeps you happy too.

So why not do yourself a favor? When the pies of life hit the floor, accentuate the positive. Instead of having a pity party, grab some spoons and start celebrating God's goodness. Have a praise party your children will never forget.

CHAPTER 10

Free to Move Forward

My mother said to me, "If you are a soldier, you will become a general. If you are a monk, you will become the Pope." Instead, I was a painter, and became Picasso.

—Pablo Picasso

His name was Jabez and the Bible sums up his entire life story in a mere two verses.

Hardly anybody had ever heard of him until a few years ago when the book *The Prayer of Jabez* hit the best-seller list. Since then, he's become something of a spiritual hero. His story has blessed and inspired people by the millions. Sermons have been preached about his bold faith. Bible studies have focused on his great vision for the future, his daring prayer, and God's answer.

Not much has been said, however, about his mother.

According to the Bible, Jabez' mom wasn't exactly an example of great positivity. Unlike other mothers I've highlighted in this book, Mama Jabez doesn't appear to be very inspirational. On the contrary, she sounds like she is dealing with negativity.

The Scriptures don't tell us how she became this way. But they do give us a glimpse into how it affected not only Jabez, but the rest of her family. In 1 Chronicles 4:9, it says:

> *Jabez was honorable above his brothers; but his mother named him Jabez [sorrow maker], saying, Because I bore him in pain.*

Short as it is, that verse reveals a lot. For one thing, it tells us that Jabez' mother named him, which means she may have been a single mom, but we don't know that for sure. (Fathers usually named their kids in those days.) It also tells us that the name she gave him was literally translated *sorrow maker*, which means she was unhappy about her circumstances and, at least to some degree, blamed Jabez for them. Finally, it tells us that his brothers were dishonorable, which often speaks to conflict or a lack of discipline in the home. Put all these factors together and we have anything but the ideal home. (Can you imagine being called Sorrow Maker all your life? Talk about an excuse for a poor self-image!)

Yet, shockingly enough, Jabez didn't end up in prison or have his name on the nation's most wanted list. Instead,

Jabez called on the God of Israel saying, "Oh, that You would bless me indeed, and enlarge my territory, that Your hand would be with me, and that You would keep me from evil, that I may not cause pain!" So God granted him what he requested.

1 Chronicles 4:10 NKJV

Isn't that amazing? In spite of his mother's mistakes and his disadvantages, Jabez turned out just fine. He grew up into a God-believing, praying man with wealth and influence and a heart to be a blessing to others.

He became such an outstanding example that God included his story in the Bible and people are still learning from him today. No matter how we get started in life, we can have a good finish if we put our trust in God.

Confessions of a Former Guilt Addict

Since Jabez' mother appeared to have no part in his success, you might be wondering why I would include her in a book about being a confident mom. So let me quickly assure you, it's not because I think we should follow in her footsteps. I'd certainly never suggest we should shrug off our responsibilities to our children and act as if our influence in their lives doesn't matter.

> *It's time we get rid of the load of guilt we often drag around and stop thinking that our mistakes are going to ruin our kids' lives!*
>
>

But here's what I would suggest: It's time we get rid of the load of guilt we often drag around and stop thinking that our mistakes are going to ruin our kids' lives!

That kind of thinking is a major problem for moms these days. Surveys show that 90 percent of mothers admit feeling guilty about not *doing* enough, *giving* enough, or *being* enough for their children.[1] Many moms even say they are wracked by guilt "most or all of the time." According to one expert, the guilt starts for the majority of mothers within days of their child being born and it never goes away. If anything, it only gets worse as their child gets older.

This is a tragedy! But as a former "guilt addict" myself, I can relate.

---

1. "Majority of mothers admit to feeling guilty for working and constantly question whether they are a good parent," *Daily Mail UK*, http://www.dailymail.co.uk/femail/article-2266292/Majority-mothers -admit-feeling-guilty-balancing-work-home-life-constantly-question -good-parent.html#ixzz2ifPOOXrB, accessed July 8, 2013.

Personally, I didn't even wait to become a mother to begin my guilt trip. I got started when I was still a child myself. As a kid, I carried a constant sense of guilt because of the sexual abuse I experienced. As children often do, I blamed myself for it.

When I grew up and began walking with the Lord, guilt continued to be my constant companion. I walked around for years saying to myself, *You shouldn't have done that! You should have done this! You ought to be ashamed!* I was even convinced such guilt was godly. I thought that if I felt badly enough about my shortcomings, I'd improve. I was also under the impression that my feelings of guilt actually pleased God—that they proved to Him I really was sorry for all the ways I disappointed Him. As a result, I didn't feel right unless I felt wrong.

But—*thank God!*—the day finally came when I realized the truth: Carrying around a burden of guilt doesn't do anybody any good at all.

It doesn't spur us on to more virtuous behavior, it makes us act worse. Guilt steals our life, day by day. It saps us of the energy we need to enjoy our family, grow in God, and be of service to Him. What's more, guilt doesn't please the Lord! It breaks His heart, because He sent Jesus to shed His blood so that we could live guilt-free.

I'll never forget the instant the full impact of this hit me. It was a defining moment in my life and it happened when I was walking across the parking lot at a Target store. As usual, I was feeling guilty about something I'd done so I was beating myself up on the inside and feeling like a worm.

Back then, the length of my guilt trip depended on how I categorized the sin I'd committed. If it was, by my own scale, just a small slip, like getting a little irritated with the kids, I might just feel guilty for a few hours. If it was a medium-sized sin, like speaking harshly or acting huffy toward them, I might feel guilty for a few days. If it was a large sin—say, I'd really chewed them out and ranted and raved—I might feel guilty for weeks.

This particular time I'd done something in the large category, so I'd been feeling guilty for quite a while and still had a ways to go. As I was walking across the parking lot, the Lord whispered to me, "How do you plan to get rid of this guilt you're carrying?"

I knew exactly how to answer. "I'll just receive the sacrifice Jesus made for me on the cross," I answered, feeling very spiritual.

"When do you plan to do that?" He asked.

I figured since He already knew anyway, I might as well be honest. "In two or three days."

"Joyce, if that sacrifice is going to be good in two or three days, isn't it also good now?"

"Yes, Lord, it is."

"Then I'd appreciate it if you'd go ahead and receive it and stop feeling guilty. Because I need you and, frankly, you're not very useful to Me in this condition!"

As I stood there in that parking lot thinking about what God had placed in my heart, I had an awakening. It fully dawned on me that the mountain of guilt I'd been buried under was depriving me and my family of the abundant, joyful life Jesus died to give us. So I rolled up my spiritual sleeves and started digging my way out. I began studying what the Bible says about God's forgiveness and grace. I renewed my mind so I could think about my sins—past, present, and future—the way He does. God forgives us completely and removes our sins as far as the east is from the west and remembers them no more!!! (see Hebrews 10:17-18, Psalm 103:12.)

Since then, I've been a different person. I have a guilt-attack occasionally like we all do, but I recognize it and refuse to live with it for very long.

If God Is Happy with You, You Can Be Happy Too

We don't have to wake up every morning feeling guilty for the messes we made yesterday and worrying about the ones we're afraid we might make today! But when I do fail in my life, I no longer let guilt weigh me down

We don't have to wake up every morning feeling guilty for the messes we made yesterday and worrying about the ones we're afraid we might make today!

because I understand three scriptural truths that every mother who wants to live guilt-free must understand.

The first truth is this: When Jesus went to the cross, He defeated sin once and for all. As Romans 8:3 says, He "...*subdued, overcame, deprived it of its power over all who accept that sacrifice.* Therefore we don't have to live in fear of it.

Instead we can do what Romans 6:11 tells us to do:

> *Consider yourselves also dead to sin and your relation to it broken, but alive to God [living in unbroken fellowship with Him] in Christ Jesus.*

In other words, we can stop focusing on our shortcomings and focus on God for a change! We can fellowship with Him instead of our mistakes. For us as moms, that means we can quit being legalists, trying to keep all the rules we've made for ourselves (i.e. Thou shalt never miss even one of thy children's softball games. Thou shalt not skip bath time and put thy children to bed with dirty feet, no matter how tired you are. Thou shalt not use Veggie Tales as a babysitter, even if it is a Christian cartoon.) And instead we can focus on growing as close as we can to the Lord, walking in love, following His leadership, and doing what He graces us to do.

"But what if I can't do perfectly what God has called me to do?"

Oh, trust me, you won't. None of us do—not by human standards anyway. But thankfully, God's definition of perfection is different than ours. According to Jesus, He defines being perfect as... *growing into complete maturity of godliness in mind and character* (Matthew 5:48). God is not really as hard to get along with as we think He is sometimes. As long as we're growing and making progress, He's happy with us.

The way I see it, if God is happy with us, we might as well stop feeling guilty that we haven't totally arrived yet and be happy with ourselves too!

I'm not saying, of course, that when we disobey the Lord and knowingly do something wrong we should just ignore our sin and act like it doesn't matter. It does matter, both to God and to us. Therefore we should admit our sins and receive His forgiveness so that we can leave that sin behind us and go on.

Which brings me to the second scriptural truth that sets us free from the guilt cycle: Jesus has already paid the whole price for every sin we'll ever commit—past, present, or future. He has already provided complete and total forgiveness for us. All He asks us to do is receive it and believe that...*he is faithful and just to forgive us our sins and to cleanse us from all wickedness* (1 John 1:9 NLT).

Notice, according to that verse, God not only forgives us, He cleanses us! He actually *came to take away our sins* (1 John 3:5 NLT). He removes them as far as the east is from the west (see Psalm 103:12) and remembers them no more (see Hebrews 10:17). Because God forgets everything we've done wrong, we're free to do the same!

I have to warn you: the devil hates this arrangement. He hates it that you can just accept the sacrifice of Jesus and go on your way guilt-free. So he'll keep trying to remind you of everything you've done wrong. He'll do his best to make you feel guilty and ashamed and unrighteous. But when he does, you can be like the believers in Revelation 12:11 who overcame the accusations of the devil by...*the blood of the Lamb and by the utterance of their testimony.*

You can say, "That sin is gone and forgotten. It doesn't even exist anymore because the blood of Jesus has wiped it out. I'm forgiven and cleansed! There is no condemnation in me!"

When you first start saying those things, your emotions might still give you trouble. You might still feel guilty. But if you'll stick with the truth of the Word, your emotions will eventually come in line and you will actually feel guilt-free!

Don't Buy the Lie

If you have made mistakes that have affected your children in one way or another, I want to encourage you to remember this third scriptural truth: There is nothing you've done wrong that is too big for God to fix. He can truly make all things work together for good, not only for you but for your children too.

Once again, I'm not proposing that you just ignore your parenting mistakes. When you do something that negatively impacts your children, you should be honest with them and acknowledge it. You should apologize to them, pray for them, and trust God to cover the situation with His mercy and grace. But once you've

> There is nothing you've done wrong that is too big for God to fix. He can truly make all things work together for good, not only for you but for your children too.

done those things, you shouldn't buy the lie that your kids can't recover from your mistakes. They can if they want to.

I'm living proof of this. I had a nightmare for a childhood. But I cried out to God, and when I was grown He resurrected what I'd lost and repaid me double for my trouble.

I saw this same miracle repeated with my own children. When they were little, because I was still in the early stages of Christian maturity and I didn't know what I do now, I passed along some of the pain of my own childhood to them. Although I didn't physically mistreat them in any way, I did a lot of yelling and was very impatient and quite legalistic.

My oldest son used to remind me of this quite often. Whenever he did something wrong he'd say to me, "If you hadn't treated me the way you did, I wouldn't be like I am!" For a while, I let his words make me feel guilty. But then one day God set me straight by reminding me of this: "Your son has the same opportunity you had. He can recover by My Word just like you did."

That message was not only good for me, it was good for him! He ultimately took it to heart and grew into a wonderful man of God. Although I still wish I'd been wiser when he was a child so that I could have been a better mom to him and my other kids, by God's grace, our family has turned out great. We all get along. We enjoy serving God and spending time together.

Now, the boys still like to tease me. When they do something I don't like, they say, "Hey, I got that from you!" When they do something good, I turn it around on them. "You got that from me too!" I say. Then we all laugh.

Our family isn't a totally unique case either. God has done the same kind of thing for many others. I know of one mom, for instance, who had some serious problems when her daughter was a child. As a result, she made some major mistakes and caused her daughter a great deal of pain. When the girl grew up, she responded to that pain by becoming an alcoholic. Bitter and angry, she continually blamed her mother for it.

Eventually, however, this mom got a revelation of God's forgiveness and grace. Determined to live guilt-free and move on with her life, she stopped allowing her daughter to berate her. She acknowledged that she'd made mistakes but she told her daughter, "You are responsible for your own choices. I'm sorry I hurt you, but if you will forgive me and take hold of the Word, you can turn your life around."

It was a tough-love conversation but in the end, things worked out well. The daughter straightened up and established a good relationship not only with the Lord but with her mom. Even though they lived in different cities, the daughter started calling her mother long distance every day just to talk.

> *We can't move forward into the wonderful future God has planned for our family as long as we're dragging yesterday's guilt and garbage behind us.*

Such stories confirm something all of us as moms need to remember: We can't move forward into the wonderful future God has planned for our family as long as we're dragging yesterday's guilt and garbage behind us.

So, no matter what we've done wrong in the past, we need to receive God's forgiveness and say like the apostle Paul did:

> *I have not achieved it, but I focus on this one thing: Forgetting the past and looking forward to what lies ahead, I press on to reach the end of the race and receive the heavenly prize for which God, through Christ Jesus, is calling us.*
>
> Philippians 3:13-14 NLT

This is the wonderful lesson we can learn from Jabez and his mom: Our mistakes don't have the power to ruin our children's future. Because of what Jesus did, we are all free to move forward.

Guilt-free.

CHAPTER 11

Dare Not to Compare

Some years ago, a couple of geese took up residence on the lake behind our house. I won't claim that God actually sent them, but I will say the timing was perfect. I was preparing to teach a seminar on parenting and, as if He wanted to provide me with a good illustration to use, the geese laid some eggs and started a family.

One day I'd been jotting down some notes about Proverbs 22:6: *Train up a child in the way he should go [and in keeping with his individual gift or bent]....* With that verse on my mind, I looked out the window to see the mother goose and her mate behaving as if they'd been studying it too.

They'd lined up all six of their fuzzy little goslings and, with one parent at the front of the line and the other at the back of the line, they were trying to train their little brood to follow the leader.

Five of the six did fine. They waddled lockstep behind

their mama and didn't miss a beat. One of them, however, insisted on being an oddball and marked out his own path. The parents kept making space for him in the line and showing him what to do. But he simply would not get with the program.

I couldn't help but laugh. All moms face that dilemma at times. We're trying to get our children to be just like us. We're saying, "Look here! We'll show you what to do and how to do it." But despite our efforts, sometimes our kids seem determined to march to a different beat. Like the oddball gosling, they just won't get with our program.

That's one reason why God told us to...*train up a child...in keeping with his individual gift or bent.* He wanted to remind us that our children are each unique, and that our calling is to discover that uniqueness and affirm it. We're anointed by God not to turn our kids into carbon copies of ourselves (or anybody else) but to strengthen their individuality.

Of course, in theory, this is what most every Christian mother wants to do. But many of us have to admit, we sometimes struggle with it.

Why? Because, as I said earlier, we can't give away what we don't have. So if we're not thrilled with our own uniqueness, if we're still comparing ourselves to other moms, trying to impress them and be like them,

we're going to pass that attitude along to our children...
whether we intend to or not.

A blog posted on the Internet recently drove this point
home. It contained the confession of a mother who, during the early years of her children's lives, had energeti-
cally pushed them to excel. She'd been so determined
they would be the best at everything—from sports, to
music, to manners, and dress—that she critiqued them
incessantly. She assumed she had only their interests at
heart. Then one day she realized the truth. What was
driving her was her own insecurity. "It was all about
me," she wrote.

> I was concerned about how my children's behavior
> or appearance was going to reflect on me. I pushed
> for perfection because I was overly concerned about
> what other people were going to think of me, not
> them.
>
> But all that changed the day my youngest daugh-
> ter laid down her ukulele in the middle of a practice
> session. After much parental scrutiny and disap-
> proval for the way she was playing, she just stopped.
> As if surrendering to a battle she could never win,
> my child said seven words I won't forget as long as I
> live. "I just want to be good, Mama."

My child, who has a genuine talent for playing the ukulele and an inherent love of singing, thought she was *no* good. And it was because of me . . . [1]

Happily, the story ended well. The mom turned things around. But I'm thankful she shared her experience because I think many moms can identify with it. I certainly can. I may not have done exactly what she did when my children were young, but I know what it's like to feel insecure and worry about what other people think. When it comes to comparing myself to other women and feeling like I don't measure up, I've been there, done that, and have the T-shirt.

As far as I can remember, I've never felt like I fit the mold of the normal mom. In fact, for years I didn't even feel like I qualified as a normal woman! For one thing, my voice is too low. Instead of having a soft, sweet, feminine voice like most ladies do, I have a voice that sounds so much like a man's that once when I called a spa to book a facial, the woman on the other end of the phone asked me if I had a beard or a goatee!

I can laugh about that now, but there was a time in my life when I would have cried about it for days. My

---

1. Hands-Free Mama, "Noticing the Good in Our Kids." *Mom to Mom*, June 25, 2013, living.msn.com. Web, accessed July 10, 2013.

voice wasn't the only thing I wanted to cry about either. I also used to grieve over my lack of domesticity. I thought something was wrong with me because I wasn't a master chef and an awe-inspiring seamstress.

Instead of celebrating my own unique bent and the gift God had given me to teach the Word, I decided during one season of my life that I should be more like my neighbor. I call her Mrs. Crafty because she was always doing crafts and planting gardens and canning tomatoes. One year, I got so set on conforming myself to her image that I talked Dave into plowing up a patch of ground in our backyard and planting tomatoes so that Mrs. Crafty and I could do some canning together.

Dave did most of the gardening work. He pulled the weeds and watered faithfully until the day finally came when my beautiful tomatoes were fully ripe. With my canning equipment all ready, I called Mrs. Crafty, and we decided to get started the following day.

But the next morning I went out to pick the tomatoes and made a horrifying discovery. A swarm of bugs had gotten into them overnight and chewed big, black holes in them. Devastated, I called Mrs. Crafty. "Our tomatoes are ruined!" I said.

She ran out to her backyard (which was just feet away from mine) to see how badly her plants had been damaged. Then she called me back and told me the *good* news. "My tomatoes are fine!"

Indignant, I hung up the phone and asked the Lord to please explain the situation. "What is the deal here?" I said. "I prayed over those tomatoes! I seriously doubt that Mrs. Crafty prayed over hers! Why did mine get ruined and hers survive?"

His answer was swift and simple: "I never told you to grow tomatoes. Therefore I have no obligation to protect your tomatoes."

Although I tell that story often, it's worth repeating here because it applies so much to us moms. Moms, perhaps more than anyone else, need to appreciate and cultivate the unique gifts and individual bent God has given us.

It can make a tremendous difference not only for us but for our children.

> *Moms, perhaps more than anyone else, need to appreciate and cultivate the unique gifts and individual bent God has given us.*

Think about that the next time you take a can of tomatoes out of your pantry. Remember Mrs. Crafty and me and say to yourself, "Doing what another mother does (no matter how much I may admire her) won't work if that's not what God created me do."

Beware of Social Envy

You might also want to remember my tomato story when you're browsing through your favorite social media websites. These sites can be a major breeding ground for insecurity. According to one researcher:

> [They] can stir up intense envy and can also negatively impact life satisfaction [because] on social networks everybody tries to come across at their best, often embellishing their profiles... *Friends* became a reference group against which one starts to compare one's own popularity and success—and this easily leads to glorifying others and putting them above oneself, i.e. the perfect recipe for feelings of envy.[2]

I'm not just picking on social media. Many other factors can be blamed too (including human nature). But the bottom line is this: There is an epidemic of insecurity among moms these days.

You as a believer, however, do not have to put up with it in your own life. You have another option because the Bible says this about you:

---

2. Fanny Jiminez, "Social Envy." January 27, 2013, worldcrunch .com. Web, accessed May 9, 2013.

> *No weapon that is formed against you shall prosper,*
> *and every tongue that shall rise against you in judg-*
> *ment you shall show to be in the wrong. This [peace,*
> *righteousness, security, triumph over opposition] is*
> *the heritage of the servants of the Lord....*

Isaiah 54:17

Notice that the verse says *security* is part of your spiritual inheritance. That means neither the devil nor anyone else has the power to make you feel insecure. You've inherited the right through your relationship with Christ to be absolutely secure in who you are.

On days when you don't feel very secure in who God has created you to be, remember that your feelings aren't the truth about who you are. God's Word is absolute truth and it says that because you're a joint heir with Jesus, whatever He has, you have. Jesus is secure, and therefore you can be completely secure in Him.

So dare to believe it! Instead of siding with your emotions, agree with what the Word says about you. Dare to say to God, like the psalmist David did, *I am fearfully and wonderfully made; marvelous are Your works, and that my soul knows very well* (Psalm 139:14 NKJV).

While you're at it, dare *not* to compare yourself to anyone else—not the other mothers at church, or your social media friends, or the magazine models with airbrushed faces and 0 percent body fat. Don't say, "I wish I looked like her...or had her talents and abilities." Don't waste your life wishing for something that you don't have. Embrace, love, and value how God created you!

As you do this, you're likely to discover that the things you dislike about yourself the most are what God uses the most, once you stop feeling bad about them. In my life, for instance, my voice has turned out to be one of my greatest assets. Because it's forceful and authoritative, it commands attention when I preach. People listen to it. These days I realize that's a blessing.

So is the fact that I don't like to cook and grow tomatoes. I don't have time for those kinds of things. I'm too busy doing everything else God has given me to do.

Oh, how much more fun life can be when we get this: God made us different on purpose! He wants us to celebrate those differences, not cry about them. Sure, some people will criticize our uniqueness. From time to time, other moms may wag their fingers about the choices we make and how we raise our kids. But if we want God's peace and joy, we can't waste our time trying to be people-pleasers.

We must find out what God's plan is for us, and our children, and follow it.

One day a mom came to me for prayer during one of my conferences. She was crying, and when I asked her what was wrong, she told me that everybody in her town homeschooled their kids. "They think it's the only way to go," she said, "but I don't have one thimbleful of desire or talent to do it. I hate it! I know if I put my kids in a public school or even in a Christian school, the other mothers will criticize me and gossip about me. What should I do?"

By now, you know how I answered. "Be yourself. Be the mom God created you to be. Use the gifts He's given you, and follow your unique, individual bent. Don't try to follow anybody else's program. Stick with God's."

Of course, you may have to work hard to remember this advice when it comes to applying it to your children. Especially if one or two of them happen to be little independent "goslings" who don't think and act the way you do. As the mother goose found out in my backyard, it's not easy to raise a child who has a personality that's the polar opposite of yours. Yet that challenge is often part of the adventure of motherhood.

For example, I have what some people refer to as a *choleric* personality. Choleric people are primarily motivated by accomplishment. We tend to be very goal-oriented, productive, serious, strong-willed, bossy, and blunt. My daughter Laura was not very motivated, got poor grades in school, and in my estimation, was messy with her personal belongings. Needless to say, she and

I had many heated arguments that involved me trying to make her be like me, but I realize now that half of the time she probably didn't even understand what I was talking about. Because of the differences in our personalities, we saw things in two different ways and our motivations in life were polar opposites. I thrived on accomplishment and she thrived on relaxation. I cared about every tiny detail of how things looked, and she didn't even notice them. Now, as an adult with four children of her own, she not only does a great job with her own family, but she helps me with many of the details of my life. Children do grow up, and with proper parenting and lots of help from God, they learn how to use their strengths and discipline their weaknesses.

My son David was very strong-willed and stubborn, and of course, we clashed because I was the same way. When two strong-willed people both want their way, someone is always going to be unhappy. Sandy was a perfectionist and Danny was a fun-loving, very energetic sanguine, so with all four of my children being quite different and me not understanding yet how to help them be who they were, we had some frustrating years. I am sure that just like I did, you have looked at your children and thought, "What planet did you come from?" It is hard at times to grasp how different they all are, but it is very important that we learn to accept our children for who they are and help them be all that God intends them to be, and not pressure them to be what we want them to be.

By God's grace, I finally learned an important lesson from the experiences I had with them: It's never a good idea to compare any child to another. It's never wise either to think or say something like, "Why can't you be more like So-and-so?" Such criticisms can lead to things like heartbreak, tears, rebellion, and insecurity.

So dare not to compare. Don't compare them to one another or to yourself. Dare to train up your child in keeping with his individual gift or bent. Even if he marches to a different beat, let him be good at being who God created him to be.

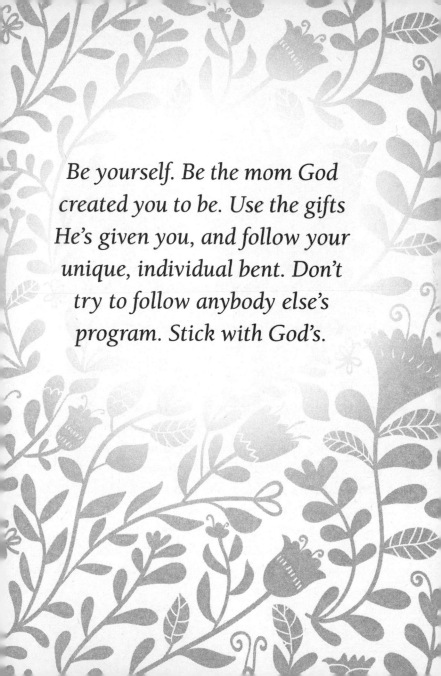

Be yourself. Be the mom God created you to be. Use the gifts He's given you, and follow your unique, individual bent. Don't try to follow anybody else's program. Stick with God's.

CHAPTER 12

What Are You Saying?

I knew when I saw my son walking toward the car after school that the test hadn't gone well. Shoulders sagging, tears brimming in his eyes, he looked the picture of defeat. Sliding into the passenger seat, he slammed the door and handed me the test paper. I could see at a glance the letter *F* glaring at me in red from the top of the page.

"Mom, what else can I do?" he cried. "I've tried everything I know. I've done my best. But I just keep failing."

My heart broke for him, but his dad and I had run out of ways to help. We'd worked with him night after night on his homework. We'd studied with him for his tests. We'd drilled him until he could answer every question perfectly. But when he got to class, the answers left his mind.

For two months, his grades had plummeted into the disaster zone. Ds and Fs had become the norm.

Although I'd asked God repeatedly to intervene, my prayers hadn't seemed to work. So when we got home, after encouraging my son one more time, I got alone and prayed yet again. "This situation doesn't make any sense, Lord!" I said. "I'm at my wits end here. I simply don't know how to turn this around!"

I didn't have to wait long for a response. Almost instantly, I heard His voice resounding in my heart.

"Call things that are not as though they were," He said. "Stop rehearsing the problem and start speaking forth the solution according to My Word!"

Do you remember the old V-8 commercials where the people slapped their foreheads when they realized they'd chosen the wrong beverage? That's what I felt like doing when I heard the Lord's answer. I wanted to slap my forehead and say, "What have I been thinking? I could have been speaking the Word over him all along!"

After all, God taught me years before how much power our words have. I could recite by heart such verses as:

- *Death and life are in the power of the tongue... (Proverbs 18:21).*

- *From the fruit of his words a man shall be satisfied with good... (Proverbs 12:14).*

- *A good man eats good from the fruit of his mouth... (Proverbs 13:2).*

- *...Whoever says... and does not doubt in his heart, but believes that those things he says will be done, he will have whatever he says (Mark 11:23 NKJV).*

- *For let him who wants to enjoy life and see good days... keep his tongue free from evil and his lips from guile (1 Peter 3:10).*

For some reason, however, it hadn't occurred to me to apply those verses to my son's situation. As a result, I'd been undoing my own prayers. I'd pray for his grades to go up, but then I'd go out and rehearse the problem. I'd sit and talk to Dave about it at night. I'd go have coffee with my best friend and say things like, "Nothing we do to help makes any difference. Our son still keeps making Ds and Fs!"

Of course, I didn't make such negative statements when my son was around, so he didn't hear them. But the devil did, and he used them as a license to perpetuate the problem. Therefore, every time I talked about it, I dug the rut deeper and made it harder for my son to get out. I actually used my words to make the situation worse. He struggled so much that he developed a fear of failing, and so between his fear and my negative confession, we were doomed to keep repeating the failure cycle unless something changed.

Thankfully, the Lord woke me up to what I'd been doing. He opened my eyes to the tremendous power I could release if I stopped using my words to hinder my son and started using them to help him. By telling me to *"call things that are not as though they were,"* He reminded me about Abram in the Old Testament.

If Abram hadn't called things that are not as though they were, his son wouldn't have even been born!

If you've read the story in the Bible, you know what I mean. Abram and his barren wife prayed for and heard promises from God about their descendants for many years, but they remained childless as long as they kept speaking the same old words. When they were both over 90 years old, however, God pulled them out of their verbal rut. He said to Abram:

> . . . *You shall be the father of many nations. Nor shall your name any longer be Abram [high, exalted father]; but your name shall be Abraham [father of a multitude], for I have made you the father of many nations.*
>
> Genesis 17:4-5

From that time on, the couple's words changed. Despite all the evidence to the contrary, they started calling Abram *Abraham, the Father of a Multitude.* At first it probably sounded peculiar to them (and all their friends and relatives), but they stuck with it anyway. They continually said about themselves what God had said…and eventually they were parents!

The Domino Effect

That's a Bible story all moms need to remember! It reveals just how much of an effect what we say has on our children—not just before they're born, as in Abraham's case, but as they're growing up as well.

> *Because of the spiritual authority God has given us over our kids' lives, the words we speak about them can either bless them or harm them.*
>
>

The Scriptures are clear about this: Because of the spiritual authority God has given us over our kids' lives, the words we speak about them can either bless them or harm them. Parental authority is a powerful thing! How we use it has a life-changing impact on our children and grandchildren for generations to come. In Exodus 20:5-6, God put it this way:

> *…I the Lord your God am a jealous God, visiting the iniquity of the fathers upon the children to the third and fourth generation of those who hate Me, but show-*

ing mercy and steadfast love to a thousand generations
of those who love Me and keep My commandments.

I don't mind telling you, those verses used to bother me. It seemed unfair that God would allow future generations to suffer because of their parents' bad choices. Especially since I experienced abuse as a child myself, I didn't understand it.

As I sought the Lord about it, He showed me that when He originally set His system of authority in place, He meant it to work for our good. He intended for parents to use their authority to enrich their children's lives and turn successive generations toward Him. But because He honors free will, He also allows each parent to choose what they're going to do.

If we choose badly and rebel against the instructions God gives us in His Word, we won't be the only ones who experience the sad consequences; our children, grandchildren, and great grandchildren will too. That's the downside of parental authority. And it's very sobering.

But there's also an upside that's far more powerful.

If we choose to love and obey the Lord, we can actually *reverse* the negative trends that were set in motion by parents and grandparents who made ungodly choices. We can start a domino effect that will bring God's holy, loving influence into our family for a thousand generations to come.

All children eventually have to choose for themselves whether or not they will follow God, but if we bring them up in a God-saturated environment, it will greatly impact their decision. If we teach them about the Lord and let them see us living in a way that reveals to them His character, if we exercise the spiritual authority God has given us by speaking words of faith over our children in accordance with the Bible, they'll become receptive to the Lord at an early age.

The influence of a godly mother who will speak God's Word over her children cannot be overstated.

Consider the young disciple Timothy in Acts chapter 16. Timothy was *the son of a Jewish woman who was a believer* (v. 1). Although his father was an unsaved Greek, Timothy ultimately became a strong leader in the early Church. Why? Because, as the apostle Paul wrote to him in 2 Timothy 1:5, ... *The genuine faith that ... dwelt first in your grandmother Lois and your mother Eunice ... is in you also* (NKJV).

Notice that in Timothy's case, it was his mother and grandmother who brought God's influence into the home. There was no Christian father to help. Timothy's mother was married to an unbeliever. Yet in Timothy's family, what Paul wrote in 1 Corinthians 7:13-14 (NLT) proved to be true:

If a Christian woman has a husband who is not a believer and he is willing to continue living with her... the Christian wife brings holiness to her marriage.... Otherwise, your children would not be holy, but now they are holy.

If you have a husband who isn't living for the Lord, let this be a comfort to you: Darkness can never overcome light. Even if your spouse is setting an ungodly example in front of your children, as you continue to do things God's way, your influence will ultimately prevail and make the difference for your kids.

Am I saying they will follow God 100 percent of the time without fail?

No, I'm not. No parent—regardless of how wonderful their influence might be—has that guarantee. After all, God was the perfect Parent and His son, Adam, rebelled against Him. In the end, however, God set things right, even with Adam. And in most every case, we can do the same with our children by taking a firm stand on the Word, keeping a positive attitude, and (even if things get a little messy and ugly for a while) continuing to believe that if we train up our child in the way he should go, *when he is old he will not depart from it* (Proverbs 22:6).

Put Your Words to Work

I was reminded the day God spoke to me about my son's grades that training up our children to go God's way involves speaking words of faith over them. In fact, that's a major part of our responsibility as parents. We are called by God to *bless* our children and not *curse* them. And in the Bible, the Hebrew word translated "bless" means *to speak well of*; and the word "curse" means *to speak evil of*.

I'll never forget what Dave said to me about this. We had been discussing what happens when parents talk negatively about their children and he told me something he'd never shared with me before.

He said that in the early years of our marriage, when I was so hard, harsh, and difficult to get along with, God made it clear to him that if he went around talking to people about my problems, the work God wanted to do in me would be short-circuited. Dave knew in his heart this was true even though he'd never heard any teaching from the Bible about the power of words. So he resolved to keep his mouth shut.

"Joyce," he said, "sometimes the way you'd act and the cutting things you'd say would hurt me so badly that I'd have to go someplace alone and cry. But I never said anything to anybody about it. I just kept believing that God would complete the good work He began in you and help you become the woman He showed me you would someday be."

Imagine how easy it would have been in those days for Dave to go to his mother, or his sister (who lived right downstairs from us) and tell them what a mess I was! But he didn't. And I'll be forever grateful because if he had, I'm not sure I'd be the woman I am today. Dave feels so strongly about this that he believes one of the most disastrous things moms and dads can do when they're having trouble, either with each other or with their children, is to talk about those problems to other people.

I don't mean to be unrealistic here. There's a balance to this. There will be times when you as a mom find it necessary to discuss with others a difficulty your child might be having. You may need to talk about the problem with your husband, your pastor, or a teacher at school to make sure your child receives the help and support he or she needs.

But even in those instances, you can speak about them in a positive way. You can bless them in the midst of their struggle by making declarations of faith that are based, not on the problems they are experiencing, but on Scriptures like these:

How joyful are those who fear the Lord and delight in obeying his commands. Their children will be successful everywhere; an entire generation of godly people will be blessed.

Psalm 112:1-2 NLT

The children of your people will live in security. Their children's children will thrive in your presence.

Psalm 102:28 NLT

And all your [spiritual] children shall be disciples [taught by the Lord and obedient to His will], and great shall be the peace and undisturbed composure of your children.

Isaiah 54:13

The mercy and loving-kindness of the Lord are from everlasting to everlasting upon those who reverently and worshipfully fear Him, and His righteousness is to children's children.

Psalm 103:17

Thus says the LORD: "Even the captives of the mighty shall be taken away, and the prey of the terrible be delivered; for I will contend with him who contends with you, and I will save your children."

Isaiah 49:25 NKJV

I'm happy to report that once the Lord reminded me of such Scriptures and told me to call things that are not as though they were, I began to make these kinds of declarations where my son's grades were concerned. Applying them specifically to his situation, I started saying, "He gets good grades. He gets As and Bs."

What happened?

My words went to work and a short time later, things changed. His grades began to improve, and although they were not perfect, they were a lot better. When I picked him up from school, he wasn't downcast and fearful anymore. One thing is for sure: making a negative comment about your children has the potential to hurt them and make their situation worse, but positive, faith-filled words never hurt anybody and are very likely to help in any situation.

CHAPTER 13

Shaping Your Child's Life

I once taught a seminar titled *Shaping the Lives of Your Children*. During one of the sessions, I asked the audience this question: How many of you were disciplined by your parents in a healthy, balanced way when you were a child? Very few hands went up.

Looking out across the group, it hit me. Many wonderful Christian parents have little confidence in their ability to discipline their children because they've had no good role model. They don't want to go down the same road their parents did, but they don't know how to find a better route.

I know what that's like. When it came to disciplining my children in my early years as a mom, I was all over the map. At one moment, I might be too strict on them because of my strong, bossy personality. The next moment, I'd be smothering them with an avalanche of sympathy because I was afraid I might hurt them like my father hurt me. I'd talk on...and on...and on...about how sorry I was that I had to correct them until I am sure they wished desperately I would stop talking and just get the correction over with.

I had a very poor example of parenting while I was growing up, and I didn't start out doing it all right, but as the Lord continued to help me, I discovered four scriptural truths that got me going in the right direction. And though I'd never claim to be an expert on this subject, I believe these truths will help you, too, as you navigate the sometimes rocky road of disciplining your kids.

1. Remember, First and Foremost, that Discipline Is Love.

As moms, we need to think about this until we get comfortable with it: Genuine love is not always sweet, tender, and gooey. It also has a tough side—a side that doesn't initially feel good to our children's emotions but yields great dividends later in their lives.

Kids need this tough kind of love every bit as much as the warm fuzzy kind but, sadly, many mothers hesitate to give it. Sometimes (as in my case) that's because they were treated too harshly themselves as youngsters and they don't want their children to experience the same pain. In other instances, it's because they're insecure and afraid their kids will get angry and reject them. And many times it's simply because administering the tough side of love is never any fun—for anybody.

Most of us found this out the first few times we took our toddlers to the grocery store. When we rolled the cart down the cookie aisle and our little darling started howling—wanting us to give them a box of cookies so that they could eat them *right now!*—we had to make a choice. What were we going to do?

Were we going to say no and risk having to deal with a full-blown temper tantrum in public, with other shoppers staring at us? Were we going to endure the inconvenience of hauling a kicking, shrieking toddler to the car to apply the correction we knew they needed? Or were we just going to cave in to his demands?

All of us, at times, have been sorely tempted to choose the latter. After all, we don't want to see our children cry. We also don't want to go through a disciplinary ordeal that makes us feel like crying ourselves. But even so, we can overrule our emotions and do the right thing if we remember that by doing so, we're following God's example. We're loving our children the way He loves us.

For the Lord corrects and disciplines everyone whom He loves, and He punishes, even scourges, every son whom He accepts and welcomes to His heart and cherishes.

Hebrews 12:6

When we withhold such discipline from our kids, we're actually being unloving toward them. By sparing them (and ourselves) the temporary discomfort involved in dealing with their bad behavior today, we're setting them up for greater pain in their tomorrows. We're teaching our toddlers, for instance, that they should never have to wait for anything; that by making demands and having a fit, they can immediately get what they want.

Such a lesson will cost them dearly in years to come.

Make sure your children don't have to pay that price. Do what's best for them. Give your children not only the tender but also the tough side of love.

> Give your children not only the tender but also the tough side of love.

And when you're tempted to avoid it because it's hard, remember that the Bible says:

> *For the time being no discipline brings joy, but seems grievous and painful; but afterwards it yields a peaceable fruit of righteousness to those who have been trained by it [a harvest of fruit which consists in righteousness—in conformity to God's will in purpose, thought, and action, resulting in right living and right standing with God].*
>
> Hebrews 12:11

We all want our children to like us and think that we are awesome, but it isn't always possible to be their parent and their best friend. If you have to choose, be sure to choose proper parenting, and then the friendship will come at the right time.

2. Discipline with Action Not Emotion

Women in general, and mothers in particular, tend to be emotional creatures. In many ways this is a wonderful thing. It helps us to be sensitive to our children's feelings so that we can give them an extra hug or word of encouragement when they need it. It makes us great at kissing skinned knees and comforting young hearts broken by first crushes.

But emotions can be a problem when it comes to discipline.

This is something I didn't realize as a young mom. When my children disobeyed and they needed to be punished, I thought I should be at least a little mad at them. So I would yell and be upset for a while. I assumed my anger would motivate them to change their behavior.

It didn't, of course, and there's a scriptural reason why: For *man's anger does not promote the righteousness God* [wishes and requires] (James 1:20). Neither does any other kind of emotional outburst. Therefore, effective discipline takes the form of action, not emotion.

My husband, Dave, unlike me, seemed to understand this from the moment we became parents. Maybe it was because as a man he's less emotional. Or maybe it

Therefore, effective discipline takes the form of action, not emotion.

was because he was more spiritually mature than I was in those days. But whatever the reason, he rarely let his feelings get involved when disciplining our kids.

Instead he would calmly sit down with them and explain to them what they'd done wrong. He'd show them in the Word why their behavior wasn't acceptable. Then he'd tell them what consequences he was going to impose. "Because you did this, you won't get to go to the movie with your friends tonight," he'd say. Then he'd hug them, tell them he loved them, and that would be the end of the interaction.

Although it didn't always leave them happy with his decision, it worked great. But for some reason it didn't occur to me to follow his example. I had to receive my own revelation about it from God. I'll never forget when it happened. I'd been studying what the Bible has to say about discipline and two verses in particular caught my attention. One of them was Psalm 119:7, where David said:

I will praise and give thanks to You with uprightness of heart when I learn [by sanctified experiences] Your righteous judgments [Your decisions against and punishments for particular lines of thought and conduct].

The other verse was Proverbs 19:18, which says:

Discipline your son while there is hope, but do not [indulge your angry resentments by undue chastisements and] set yourself to his ruin.

When I put those two scriptures together, I saw clearly for the first time that God didn't want me to discipline my children with emotion. He wanted me to be clear, just, and action-oriented. He wanted me to give them *sanctified experiences* that would help them learn to do what's right.

Almost as soon as this dawned on me, my son Danny provided me with the opportunity to put it into practice. He'd borrowed a tennis ball from his sister and, instead of returning it to her when he finished playing with it, he'd lost it. She complained to me about it and I had to decide what to do.

For once, instead of responding out of irritation or any other kind of feeling, I stopped, prayed, and thought about what action I should take. As I did, I realized that the lost tennis ball represented a weakness in Danny's character. Losing things (especially when they weren't his) had become a pattern for him. He hadn't learned the importance of taking care of other people's belongings.

I knew it wasn't in his best interest to let him continue with this pattern so I decided what the consequences of his behavior should be. Then I went to his room to inform him of them. In a calm, peaceful way, I told him that the Bible teaches us we should treat others as we want to be treated ourselves and he needed to do that by looking after other people's possessions when he borrowed them. Then I said that because he hadn't done this with Sandy's tennis ball, he would not be allowed to go fishing for a week.

Fishing was one of Danny's greatest pleasures back then, so the punishment hurt. But that was the point. I wanted him to experience enough pain that he'd remember it and be sufficiently inspired to change his behavior.

In times past, I would have felt sorry for him in this situation. I would have sympathized with him and talked sternly to him for an hour about how I wished I didn't have to punish him…and how I was only doing it for his good…and how I hoped he understood my heart…and that it hurt me more than it hurt him…and whatever else came to my mind. Then more than likely, I would have caved in after two days and let him go fishing before the week was up. In other words, the correction I gave him would have been given emotionally, and then because of emotions, I would have released him from it early.

This time, however, I simply said, "I love you," and turned to walk out, knowing in the depth of my heart that he would not go fishing for a week.

Before I reached the door, Danny stopped me in my tracks. "Mom," he said, "thank you for correcting me."

I immediately knew it wasn't just him talking. It was the Lord speaking to me through his words. It was God saying, "Good job, Joyce! You *finally* got it right!"

I'm sure the entire family was glad I did.

3. Focus on What Pleases God, Not on Your Own Personal Preferences

Here's something that's easy for us moms to forget: True discipline is about teaching our children to please God; it's not about teaching them to please us.

> *True discipline is about teaching our children to please God; it's not about teaching them to please us.*
>
>

So before we make rules and try to enforce them, we should be sure those rules are based on the Word and not just our own personal preferences. Otherwise, our children will end up resenting them and the rules will foster rebellion instead of godliness.

I got a taste of this with my daughter Laura. As a child, her understanding of neatness and order was nothing like mine. Even after she thought she'd done a satisfactory job of cleaning up her room, it looked to me like a bomb had exploded in there. So I was always dealing with her about the messes she made around the house. I got into small wars with her, not because she really did that much wrong, but because I like everything clean and straight all the time, and I wanted her to please me.

To tell the truth about it, I used to harp at all three of my older children about being perpetually clean. I constantly said, "Pick up your toys! Clean yourself up!" not because there is anything biblically wrong with having toys on the floor now and then, or having your hair messed up, but because I, personally, hated disorder and dust.

My attitude was particularly hard on my daughter Laura because she didn't even notice most of the messes I was upset about. Laura ended up going through a brief time of rebellion in high school, and although that may have happened anyway, I am sure the strain on our relationship didn't help. She just started hanging around with some kids who weren't a good influence on her; and for a while I was very concerned. However, because our relationship wasn't that great, I didn't have much credibility with her when it came to giving her advice.

Those years are long gone, of course, and today our relationship is great. Now that she has to pick up after her teenagers, I am sure she would tell you that she should have been tidier and less rebellious in those days. But looking back I can see that I played my part in her stubbornness too. It would have been wiser for me to give her more space and keep in mind the instructions in Ephesians 6:4: *Don't exasperate your children by coming down hard on them. Take them by the hand and lead them in the way of the Master* (MSG).

In other words, I might have saved both Laura and myself some unnecessary trouble if I'd focused more on helping her learn to please Jesus and less on pushing her to please me.

4. Keep Your Children under Control—without Being Controlling

The concept of keeping children under control may not be popular these days, but it's very important to God. The Bible tells about one parent who discovered this the hard way. He was a Jewish priest named Eli. In Old Testament times, he ministered in the temple along with his two sons, and he definitely didn't keep them under control. As a result, they engaged in almost unthinkable behavior. They cheated worshippers out of the offerings they brought to the Lord and did lustful things with women who came to the temple.

Eventually, the Lord ran out of patience with the situation. He passed judgment on Eli and said, . . . *I will . . . punish his house forever for the iniquity of which he knew, for his sons were bringing a curse upon themselves [blaspheming God], and he did not restrain them* (1 Samuel 3:13).

To me that used to be a puzzling verse. It seemed to contradict another passage of Scripture that says Eli did speak to his sons about the bad behavior, but they didn't listen to him. One day I asked God about this. I said, "Lord, if Eli rebuked his boys, why was he judged?"

In response, the Lord pointed out to me that all Eli did was talk. He didn't take any action. As the priest in charge of temple ministry, he could have removed them from their positions there and relieved them of their authority. But he didn't. That's why God held him jointly responsible for their sins.

Obviously, since Eli's family was in ministry, this was an especially serious situation and God had to deal with it in a severe way. It also took place under the Old Covenant, which was based on the law, white the New Covenant is based on grace through Christ. But even so, I can relate to Eli's predicament. Since I oversee a ministry myself and my children work for me, I can imagine how awful it would be to have to fire one of my children for ungodly behavior. It would be very painful and I am sure also embarrassing.

Yet that's what God required of Eli—and it shows how serious He is about keeping children under control.

Thankfully, none of us will ever have to face what Eli did. But we can learn from it. We can make sure that we do more than just talk to our kids about what they do wrong.

It's important for us to understand, however, that keeping our children under control does not mean we should be controlling. Controlling parents bring out the worst in their kids. They so dominate their children that they wind up either fanning the flames of rebellion, or making their kids so dependent on them that they never really grow up.

"But Joyce," you might say, "how do I find the right balance? How do I keep my children under control without being controlling?"

One key is to remember that you aren't the only one involved in shaping your child's life. God is also involved, and so is your child. Each participant has a part to play.

As a parent, your part is to pray for your kids and teach them what the Bible says about how to

> One key is to remember that you aren't the only one involved in shaping your child's life.

live, to set up guidelines for them to follow, determine what the consequences will be if they disobey, and follow through with those consequences when necessary. God's part is to work with your children's hearts and help them change their inward attitudes. The children's part is to choose what they are going to do.

Parents get out of balance when they try to manage all three parts of this process themselves. You can avoid that mistake by doing only your part, trusting God to do His, and letting your child choose either to change his behavior or experience the consequences.

Another way to help maintain a healthy balance is by progressively giving your children more authority over their own lives. Little by little, as they grow, start letting them make some of their own decisions. Don't try to control their every move until they're 20 years old and then suddenly put them out on their own. They won't be ready. They won't have developed the skills they need to make decisions for themselves.

"But what if they make bad choices?" you might ask. "What if they decide to wear crazy clothes to school or get a weird haircut? That could affect other people's opinions of them. Shouldn't I intervene for their own good?"

Not necessarily. Many times, kids need to make some bad decisions so they can learn for themselves how to think things through. And sometimes, they just need the freedom to express their own personality and enjoy their own unique preferences.

I had to learn this when Danny was a teenager. I'd been giving him more authority over his own life, letting him make his own choices about clothes, haircuts, friends, and such, and he decided he wanted to have his hair spiked. Dave didn't have any problem with it, but I drew the line. In my opinion, it looked stupid to have part of your hair sticking straight up and the rest of it hanging every which way.

Then I remembered how ridiculous I probably looked when I was a teenager. Like all the other girls my age, I wore a scarf on my head with the knot tied right in the middle of my chin. How dumb-looking was that? Yet I liked it, and in the big scheme of things, it made no difference.

After giving it some thought, I realized that refusing to allow Danny to get his strange haircut wasn't about keeping him under godly control; it was about me trying to control him. So I decided to let him spike his hair. Not only did it fail to negatively affect his life in any way, after a while I started liking it. Even more important, it gave Danny a sense of freedom and control over his own life that he needed at the time. Best of all, it strengthened my relationship with him.

I like what James Dobson said about these kinds of

things: "Don't throw away your friendship with your teenager over behavior that has no great moral significance. There will be plenty of real issues that require you to stand like a rock. Save your big guns for those crucial confrontations." Choose your battles wisely!

In other words, if you truly want your discipline to be effective, major on the majors. Then turn your attention to one of the hardest parts of parenting—learning to let go.

CHAPTER 14

Keeping It Simple

If not for an article recently posted on the Internet, I'd have no idea that *Pinterest stress* even existed. Nor would I be aware that 42 percent of mothers claim they sometimes suffer from this stress after visiting the website full of crafts, party themes, and recipes. But now that I know about this condition, I must say I sincerely hope you are not among the afflicted.

According to the article, symptoms of this "condition" are dreadful.[1] They include: Staying up until 3 A.M. clicking through website photos of handmade birthday party favors and mourning over the fact that you'll end up buying yours at the dollar store. Sobbing into a burnt mess of expensive ingredients that were supposed to be ador-

---

1. Lyz Lenz, "How to Raise a Kid Who Isn't Whiny and Annoying," *Huffington Post*, May 9, 2013, http://www.huffingtonpost.com/lyz-lenz/how-to-raise-a-kid-who-isnt-whiny-and-annoying_b_3248085.html, accessed July 22, 2013.

able bunny cookies for the school bake sale. Getting mad because the Valentines you did make yourself for your kid's party were outdone by another mom's. And other such traumas.

Ouch. That sounds bad. Just thinking about it might make me glad my kids grew up before Do-It-Yourself sharing websites like Pinterest were invented. It might make me thank God that in the pre-Internet days when I was trying to balance being a good mom with everything else I had to do, life was a little simpler.

It *might*...except for this fact: Life still had its challenges in those days too. It hasn't been simple for thousands of years. Human beings have been complicating it ever since they exited the Garden of Eden.

Mothers are no exception. If you doubt it, just take a survey. Ask all the moms you know if they're busy these days. Almost without fail, the answer will be, "Oh my, yes!" Then you'll hear in detail just how hectic and exhausting each mother's schedule is. It won't matter if they're stay-at-home moms, career moms, single or married, you'll find that all of us have packed our lives so full of demands and activities we couldn't possibly squeeze in one more thing.

Why, if Jesus Himself showed up and sat down at our kitchen table in the morning, most of us we wouldn't even have time to visit with Him! We'd just have to wave at Him on the way out the door and say, "Sorry, Lord. The kids

> *Why, if Jesus Himself showed up and sat down at our kitchen table in the morning, most of us we wouldn't even have time to visit with Him!*
>
>

have to be at school early for band rehearsal today, I have a presentation to prepare at the office, and after work I have soccer games and a PTA meeting to attend. I just don't have any time to spare."

It's hard to imagine actually saying such things to Jesus if He were physically sitting in your house, isn't it? But spiritually, it's what we often do. He said He'd never leave us, so He's there with us, ready to fellowship with us every day...but how often do we stop to spend time with Him?

I know what you're probably thinking. *Give us a break, Joyce! Jesus understands how busy moms are. He knows we're just being responsible and doing what we have to do.*

Maybe so. But then again, maybe that's what Martha thought too. You remember reading about her, don't you? She was the woman in Jesus' day who welcomed Him and His followers into her house and offered to host His teaching workshop.

And she had a sister named Mary, who seated herself at the Lord's feet and was listening to His teaching. But Martha [overly occupied and too busy] was distracted with much serving; and she came up to Him and said, Lord, is

it nothing to You that my sister has left me to serve alone?
Tell her then to help me [to lend a hand and do her part
along with me]! But the Lord replied to her by saying,
Martha, Martha, you are anxious and troubled about
many things; there is need of only one or but a few things.
Mary has chosen the good portion [that which is to her
advantage], which shall not be taken away from her.

Luke 10:39-42

Notice, the problem with Martha wasn't that she was busy. There's nothing wrong at all with being busy. Her problem was that she was *too busy*. And more often than not, it's our problem too.

How do we know when we're too busy?

It's easy. We're too busy when, like Martha, we don't have time to spend with the Lord. I urge you to believe God's Word that says if we seek God first, all other things will be added to us (see Matthew 6:33). If you take time to spend with God, you will find that the remainder of your time is more productive. If you don't believe me, then try it and find out for yourself.

The Secret to Starting Your Day Right

I strongly believe that the way to get each day started right is to start it with God. I love Psalm 17:15, which states that we shall be fully satisfied when we awake to find ourselves beholding God and having sweet communion with Him. Perhaps for some moms the best way to start your day with God is to do it before you get out of bed. After you wake up, lie in bed for 10 minutes and talk to God. Thank Him for helping you with your day before it ever begins.

For new mothers, let me insert a caveat here. When you have an infant that isn't sleeping all night and your entire schedule is out of control, the only time you have to devote exclusively to God might be a few minutes here and there when your baby is napping. If that's your current situation, just rest in God's mercy and grace. He has great compassion for you. He'll meet you and help you in a special way during this brief but topsy-turvy time. God fully understands our unique circumstances and situations. We all have seasons in life that require us to deviate from what might be our normal routine, but we should not let it become a lifestyle.

Having regular fellowship and time with God is the most important thing that you should do for yourself. I have even encouraged moms to pay a babysitter for a few hours each week in order to spend time with God if that is their only option. I cannot stress strongly enough the importance of taking time to be with the Lord. That is where we draw strength and wisdom for all of life's situations. The truth is that the busier we are and the more responsibility we have, the more time we need with Him.

Why is that true?

Because if you will make time with God your first priority, everything else in your life will fall into place. You'll have more divine wisdom to identify what really matters and what doesn't. You'll have more grace to do the former and leave the latter happily undone—which, all by itself, will go a long way toward simplifying your life.

What's more, instead of rushing out the door already short-tempered and snapping at the kids, you'll have more peace and patience with them. You may have to send them to school with Goldfish® Crackers to snack on instead of homemade gingerbread men—because you had your nose in your Bible rather than your mixing bowl—but you'll do it with such an extra measure of love and grace that everybody will be better off.

If you start your day off right by starting it with God, you and your family will enjoy whole new levels of peace and joy. I can confirm this from personal experience.

I spent years as a young mom going to church, attending conferences, listening to recorded teachings and learning everything I could about the victorious Christian life from preachers and other people. But I never really started living in victory until I started meeting personally with God first thing in the morning every day. I never experienced a consistent, ever-increasing joy until I aligned my life and my schedule with verses like these:

> *One thing have I asked of the Lord, that will I seek, inquire for, and [insistently] require: that I may dwell in the house of the Lord [in His presence] all the days of my life, to behold and gaze upon the beauty [the sweet attractiveness and the delightful loveliness] of the Lord and to meditate, consider, and inquire in His temple.*
>
> Psalm 27:4

> *In the morning You hear my voice, O Lord; in the morning I prepare [a prayer, a sacrifice] for You and watch and wait [for You to speak to my heart].*
>
> Psalm 5:3

> *O God, You are my God; early will I seek You....*
>
> Psalm 63:1 NKJV

"But I'm not a morning person!" you might say.

Then you might want to change your confession and ask God to help you discipline yourself to get up a few minutes early, because mornings are extremely important. The Bible indicates this again and again. It tells us that Jesus got up early in the morning and prayed (see

Mark 1:35). It says that Abraham, Jacob, and David all rose up early to seek the Lord.

Obviously, God wants us to know that how we start our day matters! Even if you prefer to read and pray later in the day, at least take a few minutes to say good morning to the Lord and tell Him that you love Him and need Him!

I believe that we all need daily time with God to fulfill His plan for our lives. Without it, we cannot be the mom, the wife, or the person He has called us to be. That's why the enemy will fight you harder over your time with the Lord than he will over anything else in your life. Your very destiny depends on it.

Once I fully grasped this, the time I spend with God each morning became non-negotiable. I'd fight a bear over it if necessary. If you would like to develop the habit of spending time with God first thing in the morning instead of planning to do it later—and then perhaps never getting around to it—you may have to stop staying up so late. Many people who cannot get up in the morning struggle because they stay up too late at night. You might need to turn the television off earlier or leave a few toys on the floor and a few dishes in the sink, but you can tackle those things tomorrow after you have had refreshing time with God. I recommend seeking God early because if we do it first, there is no way to forget it, but each of us has to find what works for us. Our goal should be to fellowship with

God all throughout the day, including and acknowledging Him in all of our ways (see Proverbs 3:5-7).

Getting Dressed Spiritually

If this concept is new to you, you may be wondering exactly what you should do during the time you spend with the Lord each day. Before I give you some suggestions, let me say this: The fact that you spend time with God at all will make a tremendous difference. So don't be overly concerned about getting it "right." Just by putting God first in your day, you're telling Him that you need Him. You're giving Him honor, and He will respond.

With that said, the first thing I like to do each day is get rid of the messes from yesterday. If I feel bad about something I said or did, or if I think I failed in some way, I acknowledge it and receive the Lord's mercy and forgiveness. As Lamentations 3:21-23 says:

> *This I recall and therefore have I hope and expectation:*
> *It is because of the Lord's mercy and loving-kindness*
> *that we are not consumed, because His [tender] com-*
> *passions fail not. They are new every morning....*

This is the wonderful thing about God's system: Days of work separated by nights of sleep make every morning a fresh start. Take advantage of that fact. Don't stay mad at yourself over yesterday's blunders.

> *You can't have a good day if you're under condemnation. So receive God's mercy and begin every day with a clean slate.*
>
>

You can't have a good day if you're under condemnation. So receive God's mercy and begin every day with a clean slate. If you start the day feeling guilty, then you will more than likely be grouchy with your children and then feel even worse about yourself. It is better to walk through the day immediately repenting for and receiving God's grace, mercy, and forgiveness anytime you sin or fail. This way you keep your spirit light and free with no burdens dragging you down.

The next thing I do is thank the Lord for everything I can think of. You can thank God that you can walk, talk, see, and hear. Thank Him that you have hot water, food to eat, and a family to get up and take care of. Beginning each day with a grateful heart sets the tone for the day. Gratitude is actually a powerful weapon that drives the enemy away!

I believe that my time with God is equivalent to getting spiritually dressed. Women will spend an hour fixing their hair, putting on their makeup, and picking out just the right outfit... but they will walk out the door without getting spiritually dressed. God's Word teaches us to put on Christ, to put on the new nature God has given us, to put on mercy, to put on love and other such things. That simply means that we can take time to set our minds in the direction of walking in the Spirit instead of running in the flesh (carnality).

Consider these Scripture verses:

Be renewed in the spirit of your minds ... clothe yourselves with the new self, created according to the likeness of God in true righteousness and holiness.

Ephesians 4:23-24 NRSV

Put on the full armor of God ... with the belt of truth buckled around your waist, with the breastplate of righteousness in place, and with your feet fitted with the readiness that comes from the gospel of peace. In addition to all this, take up the shield of faith, with which you can extinguish all the flaming arrows of the evil one. Take the helmet of salvation and the sword of the Spirit, which is the word of God.

Ephesians 6:13-17 NIV

... For you have stripped off the old (unregenerate) self with its evil practices, and have clothed yourselves with the new [spiritual self], which is ... renewed and remolded

- I operate in all the fruit of the Holy Spirit (see Galatians 5:22-25).
- I am led by the Holy Spirit (see Galatians 5:16; John 16:13).

I encourage you to expand this list to fit your own life and needs and prophesy over your future every day! You have angels assigned to you that are eager to go to work on your behalf. Since the Bible says they "hearken to the voice" of God's Word, don't let them get bored. Speak the Word and give them something to do!

I also use this time to set my heart on being a blessing to other people. I ask God to show me ways to express His love to them and build them up. At the same time, I receive extra grace and strength from the Lord to help me conquer any weaknesses and susceptibility to temptation that I've noticed in myself.

I pray especially about my mouth, since saying things I don't need to say has been a weakness for me in my life.

Jesus told His disciples in the Garden of Gethsemane, *Pray that you may not [at all] enter into temptation* (Luke 22:40). I've found that's a prayer God is always willing and able to answer. When you are weak in any area, I recommend praying about it regularly and not merely when you are in the midst of being tempted. We will all be tempted, but we can certainly trust God to help us not come into the temptation.

Present all your petitions to God, ask Him for anything you need and trust that He hears and answers prayer. Always remember that God is concerned with everything that concerns you and He wants to be involved in every area of your life. There is nothing too small or too big to talk with God about. Jesus sent the Holy Spirit to be in close fellowship with you, so invite Him into all areas of your life, not merely the ones you think are spiritual.

You can be a confident mom if you will lean on God for all things and put your trust in Him. He is your Holy Partner in life, and with Him filling your heart, you will never be alone or lack wisdom in how to raise and parent your children.

Don't forget that even if you only feel like you can spend 10 minutes each morning with the Lord, begin there. It will be so fruitful you'll soon want to give Him more. You'll be able to do it too, because as you put first things first, the unnecessary distractions, like spending too much time on social media and other things, will start to drop away. You may still be busy, but because you're not too busy to spend some time at Jesus' feet, life will become simpler and sweeter.

Just as He promised in Luke 10:42, you'll have that "good portion" no one can take away.

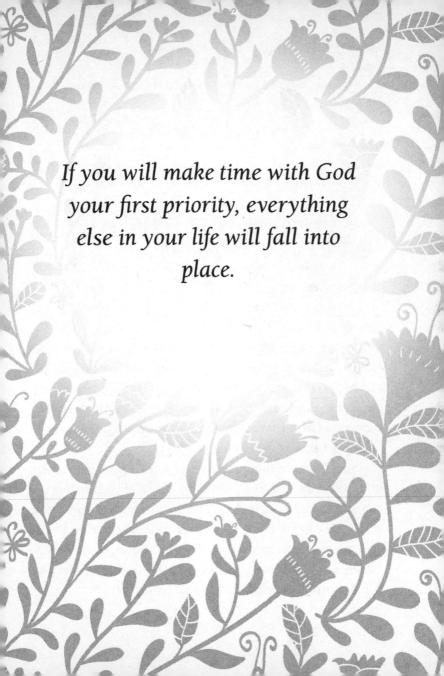

If you will make time with God your first priority, everything else in your life will fall into place.

CHAPTER 15

Enjoy the Journey

*My mother had a great deal of trouble with me,
but I think she enjoyed it.*

—Mark Twain

In the early years of World War II, a young woman named Helen tapped out a column of numbers on an adding machine. Double-checking the figures she'd entered, she made sure they were correct. Then she totaled them up and reminded herself one more time why she was doing this:

It was her way of helping the troops.

Eight hours a day, five days a week, months turned into years as she kept entering and adding…entering and adding. The numbers somehow pertained to aircrafts being built to support the war. So in theory, Helen knew she was contributing to a noble cause. But surrounded by an office full of other typists doing the same job, she also felt these three things:

Her work didn't seem very important.

Nobody was ever going to appreciate her for doing it.

And it wasn't any fun.

These insights were not unique. Helen's co-workers had caught onto them too. During coffee breaks and at lunch, they grumbled about the drudgery of their days. They pined aloud for more exciting opportunities and greater rewards. Then they trudged back to their desks and accomplished just enough to keep from getting fired.

Helen, however, chose a different approach. She decided to turn the mind-numbing task of typing numbers by the thousands into a game. Keeping track of her own speed and accuracy, each day she tried to beat what she'd accomplished the day before. She found ways to work faster and with fewer errors. She congratulated herself, celebrated her progress, and acted every day as if, by doing her job well, she could single-handedly win the entire war.

In the process, she started to enjoy herself.

She also got noticed and promoted. Which was great, but it hadn't necessarily been her goal. What Helen had set out to do was enjoy her life, every day, no matter her circumstances.

Eventually, the war ended and she married and became a mom, but she hung onto her determination. When her husband took a job that kept him out of town for long stretches of time, she transformed his absences into an adventure. She made a game out of coming up with unexpected things for her kids to do while he was gone. "Instead of eating dinner at the table tonight, let's have an indoor picnic!" she'd say as she spread a quilt on the living room floor. Or, "I know it's a school night, but let's go to a movie!"

When assigning her children chores to do, she subtly passed her attitude along to them. "If you can finish your work in an hour and do it right," she'd say, "we'll celebrate afterward."

"What will we do?" they'd ask. "How will we celebrate?"

She'd answer with a sly smile, knowing the mystery would add to the fun. "Just trust me. You'll see!"

Helen's children are grown now. They have children and grandchildren of their own. But they still revel in the memories their mom created when they were kids. They still cherish this as one of the most precious legacies she left them:

She showed them how to enjoy the ordinary moments of everyday life.

Cereal Bowls, Scrambled Eggs, and Eternal Rewards

I appreciate just how important a legacy like Helen's can be. I've had enough experience to know that for the most part, life happens in ordinary moments. Joy and fulfillment are either gained or lost by how we approach the small, seemingly mundane tasks of day-to-day life. That's why, as I close this book, I want to leave you with this challenge: Enjoy the journey of motherhood.

> That's why, as I close this book, I want to leave you with this challenge: Enjoy the journey of motherhood.

Some experts would counsel me not to say this. They claim it's unrealistic to tell women to enjoy the entire experience of motherhood. Pointing out that no one in their right mind takes delight in dealing with a teething baby or gets a kick out of scrubbing crayon marks off the walls, they warn that suggesting mothers should somehow enjoy it all puts undue pressure on them.

I realize there's an element of truth to this. And I'd never want you to feel guilty about the times you might have a tough day or get a bit discouraged. But I also believe there's a scriptural perspective that can make even mundane, repetitive tasks more satisfying. There are some things you can remember that will perk you up when the daily challenges of being a mom try to drag you down.

The first one is this: Jesus Himself notices and appreciates everything you do for your family. He attributes eternal significance to things like rinsing out cereal bowls, folding bath towels, and mopping floors that within a matter of hours will be dirty again. God always rewards faithfulness and the effort you make to serve Him with gladness.

During His life on Earth, Jesus devoted some of His most precious moments to such simple chores. In the hours before His crucifixion, for instance, He spent time washing His disciples' feet. He also made sure they didn't miss the message behind it. *And since I, your Lord and Teacher, have washed your feet, you ought to wash each other's feet. I have given you an example to follow. Do as I have done to you* (John 13:14-15 NLT).

A few days after His resurrection, He did the same kind of thing again. With only a short while left to spend with His disciples, He took time one morning to make breakfast for them (see John 21:9.) Think of it: Jesus, the resurrected King of Kings and Lord of Lords, cooking breakfast! I have to say that I absolutely love this example!!

Since He never wasted His time doing the unimportant, if Jesus washed feet and cooked meals, it was because those things matter—a lot. As a mom, you'll enjoy your life more if you'll keep this in mind. Remind yourself, when you're up to your elbows in dishwater or scrambling yet another skillet full of eggs, or under the kitchen table trying to wipe up spilled milk while trying to dodge all the feet around your head, that you're not just serving your family, you're pleasing Jesus. You are showing love to them the way He does, and you're doing exactly what He wants you to do. Love is not merely theory, or a word that we use, but it is action manifested in practical and beneficial ways.

Because you may not get much appreciation for it from those around you, here's another thing you should keep in mind: With every act of loving service, you're stacking up eternal rewards. Society may not applaud you and much of your work may go unnoticed, but according to the Bible, God keeps track of everything you do. So—

Whatever may be your task, work at it heartily (from the soul), as [something done] for the Lord and not for men, knowing [with all certainty] that...you will receive the inheritance which is your [real] reward. [The One Whom] you are actually serving [is] the Lord Christ (the Messiah).

Colossians 3:23-24

The last thing I encourage you to remember is this: Jesus came so that you can...*have and enjoy life, and have it in abundance (to the full, till it overflows)* (John 10:10). So take Him up on His offer. If anybody knows how to celebrate the ordinary moments of life, Jesus does. He's the One who turned the water into wine at the wedding of Cana to keep the party going. He's the One behind all the feasts and celebrations the Israelites enjoyed for thousands of years.

So ask Him to show you how to make everyday life more fun—for you and your children. Let Him teach you, like He taught a young woman during WWII, how to enjoy the journey of life so much that you can pass your joy along to future generations.

"Can I be confident He'll do that for me?" you might ask.

Absolutely!

CONCLUSION

As you turn these final pages in *The Confident Mom*, let me be the first to say *Congratulations! You did it!*

I'm congratulating you not just because you're a mom who finished a book (though with your busy schedule, that is a huge accomplishment!), but also because you're a mom who has successfully embarked on a new journey.

You see, the path of parenthood was never meant to be walked with anxiety or apprehension. You were not created to agonize over every misstep, second-guess every turn along the way, and freeze at every fork in the road. A mom's journey is a gift from God, and God's gifts are never to be feared—only celebrated!

I pray that this book has given you the confidence to begin celebrating again.

Regardless of where you find yourself along the trail of motherhood, let me encourage you to enjoy every step from this point forward. The excitement of pregnancy, the trials of teething, the first day of school, the summer adventures, the lessons of discipline, the late night talks, the college visits, and the transition into adulthood…it can all be lived with joy and an unshakeable confidence that God is in control.

The Word of God says, *For God did not give us a spirit of timidity (of cowardice, of craven and cringing and fawning fear), but [He has given us a spirit] of power and of love and of calm and well-balanced mind…* (2 Timothy 1:7). This is a "mom verse" if ever there was one! *Timidity, cringing,* and *fear* are things of the past! *Power, love,* and *calm* are in store for your future!

I believe today is a new day for you and for your family. God will give you new power as you fight for your children, new love in your home and your relationships with one another, and a new calm as you seek Him for His guidance in every parenting decision.

I urge you to believe that your job of being a mom is one of the most important jobs in the whole world. After all, without moms none of us would even be here. So do your job confidently and joyfully, and believe with all of your heart that you and God are in partnership in parenting and nurturing the next generation of mighty men and women of God.

Don't waste another moment. Your new journey has begun. From this day forward, celebrate your life as *The Confident Mom* God created you to be!

ABOUT THE AUTHOR

JOYCE MEYER is one of the world's leading practical Bible teachers. Her TV and radio broadcast *Enjoying Everyday Life* airs on hundreds of television networks and radio stations worldwide.

Joyce has written more than 100 inspirational books. Her bestsellers include *God Is Not Mad at You*; *Making Good Habits, Breaking Bad Habits*; *Do Yourself a Favor...Forgive*; *Living Beyond Your Feelings*; *Power Thoughts*; *Battlefield of the Mind*; *Look Great, Feel Great*; *The Confident Woman*; *I Dare You*; and *Never Give Up!*

Joyce travels extensively, holding conferences throughout the year, speaking to thousands around the world.

JOYCE MEYER MINISTRIES
U.S. & FOREIGN OFFICE ADDRESSES

JOYCE MEYER MINISTRIES

P.O. Box 655
Fenton, MO 63026
USA
(636) 349-0303

JOYCE MEYER MINISTRIES—
CANADA

P.O. Box 7700
Vancouver, BC V6B 4E2
Canada
(800) 868-1002

JOYCE MEYER MINISTRIES—
AUSTRALIA

Locked Bag 77
Mansfield Delivery Centre
Queensland 4122
Australia
(07) 3349 1200

JOYCE MEYER MINISTRIES—
ENGLAND

P.O. Box 1549
Windsor SL4 1GT
United Kingdom
01753 831102

JOYCE MEYER MINISTRIES—
SOUTH AFRICA

P.O. Box 5
Cape Town 8000
South Africa
(27) 21-701-1056